MW00529477

HOW TO BUILD A HIGH-PERFORMING SINGLE-FAMILY OFFICE

HOW TO BUILD A HIGH-PERFORMING SINGLE-FAMILY OFFICE

Guidelines for Family Members and Senior Executives

Russ Alan Prince and Robert Daugherty

gatekeeper press
Columbus, Ohio

The views and opinions expressed in this book are solely those of the author and do not reflect the views or opinions of Gatekeeper Press. Gatekeeper Press is not to be held responsible for and expressly disclaims responsibility of the content herein.

How to Build a High-Performing Single-Family Office:
Guidelines for Family Members and Senior Executives

Published by Gatekeeper Press
2167 Stringtown Rd, Suite 109
Columbus, OH 43123-2989
www.GatekeeperPress.com

Library of Congress Control Number: 2020950489

ISBN (hardcover): 9781662907388
eISBN: 9781662907395

DISCLAIMER

Dedication

Russ Alan Prince

To Jerry
Remember, every joke becomes a life lesson
Love, Dad

Dedication

Bob Daugherty

For Mary Ann, Jackson, Ben & Ella
Family first and always.

Contents

Part III:
The Family in the Single-Family Office

Appendices

Foreword

W̲E̲ ̲K̲N̲O̲W̲ ̲T̲H̲A̲T̲ people, systems, and optimal resources are the leading factors in high-performing single-family offices, however I've never seen this so tactically and eloquently broken down in actionable advice as Russ and Robert do in 'How to Build a High-Performing Single-Family Office: Guidelines for Family Members and Senior Executives.'

More than the tactical skill of the executives and those that service the family commonly through the family office, is the interplay as Russ and Robert call the human element. Understanding the most important goals and the biggest worries of the family. It takes skillful emotional intelligence and communication to uncover true goals and worries of the family.

Russ and Robert understand that how the family 'feels' about their professionals and those advisors around them, is as important as the quantitative results of their actions and solutions. 'How to Build a High-Performing Single-Family Office: Guidelines for Family Members and Senior Executives,' sets a framework for quantitative and qualitative best practices in the opaque community of single family offices.

Building a cohesive interwoven team of inside and outsourced professionals, communicating protocols and expectations, clarifying goals, enhancing systems and being clear on expectations, sharing in progress and setbacks is the only way to withstand shocks to the game plan and adapting for optimal results, is the only way this can work in a high-performing environment.

Most single family offices and those that service the community are not optimized by the very nature of statistical analysis. 60% are in the middle, 20% are superior and 20% are inferior to an average. Those that are not superior (80%) think they are in the top 20%! The principles that Russ and Robert discuss help to provide a roadmap to improvement, and not accepting of mediocrity.

I learned so much from reading this book and highly recommend it to wealth holders, family office executives and those that service the community.

—**Angelo Robles**
Founder & CEO, Family Office Association
Host of the Angelo Robles Podcast

Is This Book for You?

FAMILY OFFICES ARE garnering tremendous attention from successful families the world over. They are increasingly seen as the best way for these families to manage their wealth, deal with a wide array of non-financial issues and concerns, and help ensure their affluence transfers efficaciously to future generations.

More and more, family offices are perceived as the way these families can get *superior results*. They are being chosen over more traditional competitors such as private banks, wealth managers, law firms, and accounting firms.

The ability of a family office to produce superior results is very much dependent on YOU!

For our purposes, you are a senior executive in a family office, or you have been asked by a successful family to help them establish a single-family office. You are part of the single-family office *inner circle*. This means . . .

- You are meaningfully involved in decision-making at the single-family office

- You are meaningfully responsible for the performance of the single-family office

- You may or may not be a family member

- You are probably a technical expert, but this may not be the case

Our aim with this book is to give you critical perspectives and processes you can use to build a high-performing single-family office. There is incredible demand today for capable and talented individuals who can deliver what successful families want and need. Not only will you be delivering value to families, working in a single-family office can be very rewarding to you as well.

In order to garner the rewards you deserve, you likely will have to take steps that verify your value. Delivering greater value to the family will often lead to greater compensation. To this end, we will discuss how non-family professionals are hired to work in single-family offices and how they are compensated. We will also discuss compensation if you are a family member and part of senior management.

We derive our recommendations from extensively working with successful families over decades and in all manners of family offices. Our perspectives are grounded in research (see Appendix A). However, we are not going to be talking about empirical findings. Instead, we are going to concentrate on giving you a way of thinking about your role. We are going to give you processes to help you build a high-performing single-family office. We will also discuss how to translate your achievements for the family into greater personal success.

This is very much a "how-to" book. Within are step-by-step processes and procedures that you can use to produce a high-performing single-family office. We also provide guidance on how to better deal with certain family circumstances in order to get superior results.

So, if you are in senior management at a single-family office and are in the inner circle or want to be, this book is indeed for you.

While this book is written for inner-circle single-family office senior executives, it can also be beneficial to professionals and other providers who want to work with single-family offices. By understanding what it takes to become a high-performing single-family office, by understanding how single-family office senior executives think and how they negotiate, you can better ensure your expertise and capabilities are in sync with the ways decisions are often made.

Again, the book is first and foremost for senior executives who are part of the single-family office's inner circle. It is a "how-to" book that provides you with ways to make a single-family office high-performing and benefit accordingly. Still, it is up to you to make it happen. When you make it happen, the value to the family as well as the value you receive can be astounding.

PART I

The Fundamentals

CHAPTER 1

Family Offices

It sometimes seems that all successful families want a family office. Even families and individuals that are meaningfully less affluent want the many advantages of a family office.

The appeal of a family office, throughout the world, is considerable. In the United States, where the family office industry is in many ways more well established, new variations are making the benefits of a family office available to a broader and less financially accomplished population. At the same time, family offices and the wealth they control and oversee are growing at a tremendous and—in some cases—a near exponential rate.

With all this interest and attention, one of the biggest complications is that families and professionals are not all referring to the same thing when they say *family office*.

What's in a Name?

When you think of a family office, what comes to mind? The term "family office" is bandied about a lot and is likely to become even more widely used as more families as well as more professionals embrace the concept. The potential monkey wrench in the works is that family offices are best thought of as a category as opposed to a particular thing. That is why there is no generally accepted definition of a family office, which in turn leads to a plethora of structures, approaches, and different versions all being called a family office.

When the phrase "*family office*" is used, it can mean . . .

A single-family office is a separate legal entity dedicated to optimizing the financial and related world of one successful family. To have a single-family office, the family commonly has to have significant wealth outside their family-run business interests. The cost of operating such an entity varies extensively. The more the expertise is housed within the single-family office, the more it costs to run. A single-family office is considered the best way for a successful family to achieve superior results as well as maintain the greatest amount of control.

There are variations on a single-family office . . .

An embedded family office is often encased within a family business. A group or unit in a family business provides the family some or many of the services of a single-family office. Embedded family offices are rarely defined as family offices. Instead, they are seen as people within the family business that help the family address certain matters, including tax planning and compliance and sometimes investment management. Where possible, the costs of the embedded family office are covered by the family business.

A hub-and-spoke single-family office is a way for different family members to take control of certain aspects of their financial lives while mitigating the costs of having their own single-family office. In this model, a central single-family office delivers a range of wealth planning, administrative, and lifestyle expertise (the hub) where different family members or family branches manage their own investments (the spokes). Sometimes, investment opportunities are shared among the spokes.

A single-multi-family office is the combination of a small number of single-family offices initially in the service of unrelated families. What tends to happen is that multiple smaller (as measured by assets being managed) single-family offices with an aligned investment philosophy and a desire to offer more capabilities merge in order to increase their investment clout, deliver greater value, and mitigate costs. The single-multi-family office is not to be confused with a multi-single-family office.

A limited single-family office provides only selected expertise such as investment management. For example, a number of hedge funds have turned into single-family offices. What they are doing is disgorging themselves of clients and only managing the monies of the founder(s). Limited single-family offices are usually private investment companies. Many times, these entities end up adding on other capabilities, with some of them becoming comprehensive single-family offices.

A communal family office is where a single-family office is created for a group of closely aligned non-family members such as a religious organization. While the people involved are not connected by blood, they consider themselves family. Their resources are pooled and they often operate in ways that resemble a family. Their single-family office tends to operate just as it would if there was only one family involved. While communal family offices are not all that common, there has been a pretty steady increase in their numbers over the last few years.

The other broad category of family offices is the multi-family office . . .

A traditional multi-family office provides a suite of deliverables characteristic of a single-family office to a number of families. In most cases, multi-family offices are an extension of the wealth management model. The aim is often to work with fewer, but wealthier clients. Certain expertise is in-house and it often generates a substantial amount of the firm's revenues.

A virtual family office is a bespoke arrangement where several professionals and other providers are coordinated by one professional on behalf of a family or individual. The aim is to mirror a single-family office as much as possible. There is a meaningful but nuanced difference between a traditional multi-family office and a virtual family office. The former tends to have a much broader set of in-house expertise. In contrast, with a virtual family office, some of the expertise comes from the professionals coordinating the virtual family office, but most of the services and products are outsourced.

An outpost family office is a traditional multi-family that serves the needs of different families only when they are in a particular geographic area. A common reason to engage an outpost family office is when a successful family has a single-family office in one country and some of the family's children are going to school in another country. Instead of building some sort of support system for the children in the new country, the family engages a multi-family office geographically close to the school. Outpost family offices are also often used when a family is conducting business dealings in countries besides their own.

A family office practice is where a professional firm provides its expertise, and mostly only its expertise, to a successful family. The services and products provided are usually a subset of what a single-family office would often provide. For example, there are many accounting firms delivering tax services including planning, bill paying, financial statements, and so forth that refer to this group in their firm as their family office practice. Some investment managers focus 90% of the energies on running money and 10% on other client matters and refer to themselves as a family office. Most family office practices are delivering a small set of expertise compared to what a single-family office might provide, however this is rapidly changing. More than ever, family office practices are more closely resembling virtual family offices.

What is clear is that the term *family office* can refer to different structures and different ways of serving successful families.

In extensively researching single-family offices, for example, we defined a single-family office as:

- A separate, legal, stand-alone entity
- Providing investment management services where the senior executives are directly involved
- The one family and the senior executives identify the entity as a family office

While this definition made it much easier to conduct the research and compare the respondents, we recognize it excluded a wide array of other types of family offices. Because investment management was part of the definition, we recognized it excludes many single-family offices. To be able to put all types of family offices under the same tent, it is often useful to think of a high-performing family office in terms of its core characteristics.

Core Characteristics of High-Performing Family Offices

While our focus is on single-family offices, the following are three core characteristics of ALL high-performing family offices no matter the type (Exhibit 1.1). As an inner-circle single-family office senior executive, you have to make certain these qualities are solidly present for your single-family office to be high-performing.

EXHIBIT 1.1: Core Characteristics of High-Performing Family Offices

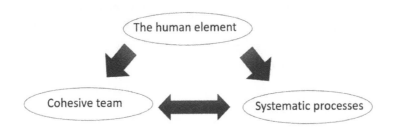

The human element: This is one of the most powerful and consequential drivers of value in the entire private wealth industry. To achieve optimal results, solutions must be spot-on. The only way that is consistently possible is if you and the other inner-circle senior executives, as well as the internal and external experts involved, truly and deeply understand the family, from their most important goals to their biggest worries.

Questions to consider:

Do you really understand the family members as people, including their hopes and dreams, concerns and anxieties?

Are you good at explaining complex concepts, ideas, opportunities, and solutions to family members and other people?

Do you have a sincere and trusting relationship with family members?

A cohesive team: To get the best outcomes possible, a team of experts adeptly supported by staff is essential. Some team members might be employees of a single-family office, while others are engaged as necessary. What is critical is that all the team members work together effectively and efficiently to deliver the greatest value possible—which is why the team is defined as cohesive.

Questions to consider:

Are you able to consistently access best-of-class expertise and solutions?

Are you invariably able to attain the expertise the family needs and wants on an expedited and exceptionally cost-effective basis?

On behalf of the family, are you able to "jump the line" when it comes to getting the solutions they need and want?

Systematic processes: Often, professionals haphazardly deal with their clients. Unfortunately, the same can be said of a percentage of inner-circle senior executives running single-family offices. Their working arrangements, for example, are far from smooth. These professionals and senior executives are not methodical in how they deal with the families to the detriment of these families.

The use of systematic processes enables the professionals and senior executives to more consistently deliver value.

Questions to consider:

Are you constantly taking steps to catch and correct any mistakes or potential problems with what the family is doing or is considering doing?

Are you regularly making certain that possible disasters will not derail the single-family office?

Are you making sure the family is staying on track and following the best possible course of action or determining whether an alternative course of action would be more appropriate and effective?

By thinking about family offices in terms of these three core characteristics, it becomes easier to understand all the variations. There are methods and approaches that tie to each core characteristic of ensuring the family office is high-performing. In the next section, we will take a deep dive into each of these core characteristics.

Conclusion

The concept of a family office can be pretty vague. Many times, it depends on who you are talking with. Nevertheless, there is extensive and expanding interest in family offices. While the wealthy are trending to choose family offices over other types of providers, those less affluent are also increasingly looking to work with some form of family office. Given their druthers, it is fair to say that nearly everyone wants to work with a high-performing family office, even if they are not completely sure what that means.

There are three core characteristics of all high-performing family offices—intense attention to the human element, a cohesive team, and a reliance on systematic processes.

Family offices in general provide a range of expertise. In the next chapter, we will discuss that range.

CHAPTER 2

The Expertise Provided by Single-Family Offices

T HERE IS CERTAINLY a burgeoning amount of information being produced about family offices. Relatively less so when it comes to single-family offices, but still a considerable quantity. Much of the research and information about single-family offices concentrate on the mechanics, such as:

- What single-family offices are investing in today
- The use of family mission statements, value statements, and constitutions in governing the single-family office
- What senior executives at family offices are paid
- The breadth and depth of special projects as well as how they are implemented by single-family offices
- How to use a private foundation to benefit the world and advance family harmony
- Particular financial and legal strategies and techniques

- The nature of particular investment strategies and opportunities from private equity to alternative investment funds to more traditional portfolios

- The nuts-and-bolts of administrative services

- How different forms of wealth planning can create differential advantages

- Determining the more and less appealing lifestyle services and how they integrate into a single-family office

While we too have often researched these topics and even consulted on many of them, they do not inherently produce a high-performing single-family office. The three core characteristics we introduced in the previous chapter adeptly implemented coupled with an ability to navigate family issues will be critical in building a high-performing family office.

Before we address how to move from a single-family office to a high-performing single-family office, it is important to be clear about what a broad-based single-family office provides.

Expertise Provided by a Single-Family Office

Generally speaking, single-family offices tend to provide two major categories of expertise—wealth management and family support (Exhibit 2.1). Wealth management consists of investment management and wealth planning. Family support tends to include administrative and lifestyle services, as well as special projects.

EXHIBIT 2.1: Expertise Provided by Many Single-Family Offices

Wealth Management	Family Support
Investment management • Discretionary investment accounts • Private equity and venture capital investments • Passion investments **Wealth planning** • Income tax planning • Estate planning • Business succession planning • Asset protection planning • Charitable tax planning • Cross-border planning • Life management planning	**Administrative services** • Tax compliance • Bill paying • Financial statements **Lifestyle services** • Concierge medicine • Family/personal security • Philanthropic advisory **Special projects** • Adoptions • Buying an island • Overseeing the construction of a house • Aircraft acquisition • Overseeing family construction projects

Within these categories are a number of different services or products. For example, there are various ways to manage money, as there are various wealth planning specialties. Administrative and lifestyle services are also umbrella categories for numerous products and services. And, special project can mean just about anything. The sheer scope of possibilities and combinations means that unique and thorny issues can be addressed in new and wholly customized types of single-family offices without deviating from the basic operating structure.

Let us dig a little deeper into each of the categories.

Investment Management

Central to a large percentage of single-family offices is investment management. There are discernible patterns when it comes to what single-family offices invest in, but these patterns can change easily as social, economic, and family circumstances change.

Today, for example, many single-family offices are directing funds to private companies. They make direct corporate investments in a number of ways, including:

- Independently buying portions or companies on their own

- In conjunction with consortiums of other single-family offices and ultra-wealthy individuals often called "club deals"

- Side-by-side investments with institutional investors such as private equity firms and sovereign wealth funds

However, this can readily change if other possibilities are likely to produce greater risk-adjusted returns.

Some single-family offices are heavily invested in passion

investments such as artwork, numismatics, and antiques. At one single-family office we worked with, one-third of the investable assets are in precious stones, one-third in alternative investments, and the rest in US Treasuries. Another single-family office built an underground vault to store more than 2,000 rare coins and a small mountain of gold and platinum bars. Other single-family offices are investing and sometimes taking equity positions in hedge funds. Most single-family offices, for the most part, are open to just about all legally sanctioned possibilities.

A distinct advantage of single-family offices, compared to many other types of investors, is that they can have longer-term investment horizons. In some cases, their investment horizons are generational or even multi-generational.

A critical consideration for the family is which financial assets are to be aggregated and which financial assets are to be managed separately by family members. This often proves to be a bigger issue for subsequent generations. Sometimes, the decisions that have been made as assets are locked in trusts. But when there is the possibility of family members controlling financial assets, the question is why is it better to keep the wealth together under the umbrella of the single-family office.

Wealth Planning

For some successful families, wealth planning is much more consequential than investment management. It can certainly deliver more predictable outcomes. From legally mitigating taxes to protecting wealth to doing the most good and ensuring continuity of the family and the family fortune, wealth planning can be crucial to building a high-performing single-family office.

The following are the most common specialties within wealth planning:

- **Income tax planning** focuses on legally mitigating taxes on money earned by working.

- **Estate planning** involves using legal strategies and financial products to determine the future disposition of current and projected assets.

- **Marital and related relations planning** entails planning for disruptions in the relationships between spouses and other lovers with the intent to protect the family's wealth.

- **Business succession planning** principally deals with tax-efficiently transitioning businesses to others, whether they are family or not.

- **Asset protection planning** entails employing legally accepted concepts and strategies to ensure that a family member's wealth is not unjustly taken from him or her.

- **Charitable tax planning** enables tax-efficient philanthropy.

- **Cross-border and inbound planning** is for family members who are operating businesses in different countries or are moving to different countries so that they facilitate business opportunities and minimize the taxes that are owed.

- **Life management planning** addresses an array of concerns from a wealth management perspective such as how to best structure wealth to deal with the concerns of longevity.

Although we are differentiating among the planning specialties, in practice there is considerable overlap as well as synergistic possibilities. Senior management at high-performing single-family offices routinely look for ways to take advantage of these overlaps and complementary possibilities.

Administrative Services

Administrative services tend to be very straightforward and mechanical but often serve a critical role. They include:

- Dealing with all tax compliance matters, including filing tax returns, audit defense, estate and gift tax execution, tracking, and administration
- Developing and updating the family balance sheet
- Producing income and cash flow statements
- Providing budgeting plans
- Bill paying and expense reporting
- Tracking and reporting investments, including addressing cost and tax basis
- Bookkeeping

When it comes to administrative services, the single-family office is the chief financial officer of the family. Even though these services can be considered straightforward, they can be complicated and must be implemented well.

Lifestyle Services

These are non-financial and non-legal services that benefit the family. Of great concern to most families is healthcare. This concern often translates into connecting family members with exceptional concierge medical practices and overseeing the ongoing relationship. Almost everyone wants to live a long, healthy life. Many successful families are looking to concierge medicine for comprehensive longevity initiatives, which entails integrating wellness, medical care, cutting-edge solutions, and astute wealth management.

Family security is also very important to successful families. Family security firms provide a range of services such as:

- Privacy and cyber protection
- Personal protection services
- Travel safety and security
- Investigations and due diligence
- Protection for property and valuables

Another lifestyle service is philanthropic advisory. Here, experts are engaged to help family members think through who they want to benefit from their largess. It not only deals with what charities to support, but includes monitoring how gifts are used and the impact they produce. Philanthropic advisory and charitable tax planning are different but complementary services.

Special Projects

High-performing single-family offices engage in one-off project management. Some examples of special projects include:

- Facilitating an adoption from another country
- Buying an island

- Arranging for experimental stem cell treatments in a foreign country
- Overseeing the construction of a 60,000-square-foot mansion
- Arranging the paperwork and facilitating the process for admissions to a private club
- Supervising the forensic accounting work for a divorcing family member
- Arranging for a family member to be "disconnected" from a self-harm site and to then receive top-quality treatment
- Restoring the identity of a family member after her company was hacked
- Arranging for underage children to be extracted from a cult

This list of one-off projects can go on and on. When it comes to special projects, external experts are always brought in and the single-family office acts as coordinator and monitor.

Delivering Synergistic Outcomes

The attractiveness of single-family offices is that they can generate synergies among the expertise they provide. By combining their focus on the family—the human element— with the vast range of potential services and products, just about anything the family wants is potentially available. Because of this approach, single-family offices continually prove themselves better than other types of financial and legal providers.

Successful families, for example, can usually benefit in various ways from the combination of investment management and wealth planning. One commonly employed possibility is the elimination of all taxes on the gains produced by an investment portfolio.

Special projects are another area where wealth planning can be highly synergistic. From the buying and selling of private islands (or private jets or yachts) to facilitating adoptions to paying for unique services most tax efficiently, wealth planning can often significantly contribute to the results families seek.

Conclusion

Family offices provide a variety of services and products to families. We presented a typology that is useful in getting an understanding of the types and range of expertise delivered by single-family offices as well as the other types of family offices. Out typology is certainly not the only one, or necessarily the best one there is. It is a way to help you think about what single-family offices do for successful families.

What is important to realize is that single-family offices can generate synergies among the services and products. However, to achieve synergies—to get the results the family is looking for—requires a high-performing single-family office. We explain why this is the case in the next chapter.

CHAPTER 3

The High-Performing Single-Family Office

THE ABILITY TO provide the various forms of expertise for one successful family can lead to the establishment of a single-family office. However, that does not mean that a single-family office is high-performing.

In researching single-family offices, we have been able to differentiate those that are high-performing and those that are not. What follows is a simplified description of the analytic method we employed to segment single-family offices:

- **Determine the family's self-interests, including their expectations concerning each type of expertise their single-family office provides**: This will specify how the family decides if they received substantial value or not. Always remember that value is not objective as value in the eyes of family members based on their expectations.

- **Compare the family's self-interests to what actually occurred**: There might be a difference between what the family anticipated will occur and what happens.

It is, therefore, necessary to have viable comparisons between their self-interests and expectations and what the single-family office has provided.

- **Statistically characterize the performance of the single-family office by creating an aggregate measure of the difference between expectations and outcomes:** The more the family's self-interests and outcomes match up with what their single-family delivered, the more that single-family office is high-performing. It is important to recognize that single-family offices can be high-performing overall, and they can be high-performing in particular areas such as investment management or administrative services.

You can use a tactical variation on this research methodology to build a high-performing single-family office (see below). Before we go there, it is useful to be clear about the inherent nature of single-family offices and the underlying rationale for their existence—the family office promise.

The Family Office Promise

When we asked family members why they set up single-family offices, we received a range of answers. In many cases, the answers were fairly consistent, such as:

- The ability to be in total control of their financial lives

- Being able to better leverage their wealth to get the highest quality non-financial services

- Ensure tight oversight of the professionals they employ
- Enable them to effectively address their family's agenda
- Better preserve their confidentiality
- Ensure family financial security for generations
- Better able to use multiple jurisdictions to legally minimize taxes
- Make sure the plethora of advisors they are relying on are well-coordinated
- Encourage entrepreneurship among family members
- Gain greater access to high-quality investments and business opportunities
- Prepare the next generation to handle substantial money
- Build, preserve, and protect the family legacy
- Put some structure into the family finances, which are presently disorganized and confusing
- Keep the family together for generations
- Increase the family's social capital; their commitment to the community and society
- Educate and professionally develop family members
- Achieve economies of scale
- Share the family's accumulated intellectual capital

When we dig deeper, we find that founders of single-family offices often see their decision to establish a single-family office in comparison to other alternatives such as private banks, law firms, and accounting firms. In this context, there is one overriding reason for these families to establish a single-family office—*superior results.*

Superior results: Bottom line: the family office is intended and expected to help deliver a *constrained optimized life.* That is the promise of a single-family office. It fulfills this promise by producing **superior results.** Whatever the self-interest of family members, the family office is perceived as the best way to achieve those self-interests and more.

Who does not want to optimize their financial situation or their ability to get state-of-the-art medical care or to legally mitigate every tax possible? We suspect that few people are not in favor of an optimized life—of getting superior results.

We say getting an optimized life is "constrained" because families—for better or worse—put restrictions and demands on their circumstances. Therefore, superior results are the best outcomes possible, within limitations, many of which are set by the family.

Consider the family that chooses to treat all next-generation family members equally. This is a constraint. It might be a good idea or a bad idea or something in between. That is not the point. It is the family's decision. As such, it places certain limitations on what constitutes superior results.

What about the family that will only invest in socially responsible companies? Again, this is a constraint. How about the family office that has to run every possible investment by the founder who tends to take months before making a decision? Again, this is constraint.

The range of deliverables of a family office is another constraint. If, for example, the family office concentrates exclusively on wealth management, the ability to facilitate an adoption or buy an island or ensure the safety of a self-destructive wayward child are—by design—outside their capabilities. All family offices are working with constraints.

Some constraints can be beneficial, while others range from slightly advantageous to innocuous to deleterious. It is within these limitations that the family office strives to deliver superior results. When the family office does indeed consistently produce superior results, it is referred to as high-performing.

Fulfilling the Family Office Promise

In your role as an inner-circle senior executive in a single-family office, the family office promise is ever-present. Seen from a different angle, fulfilling the family office promise means meeting or exceeding the self-interests of the family. In this way, you are justifying the existence of their single-family office and your role at the single-family office.

What we want to make clear is that a high-performing single-family office is high-performing, only if the family thinks it is. What we are describing is NOT a tautology. The single-family office must meet or exceed the criteria the family sets and the expectations the family has. What other people outside the family members the single-family office serves think or what some objective analysis says does not determine if a single-family office is high-performing.

High performance is determined by the single-family office doing a solid if not exceptional job of helping the family achieve its self-interests.

Failing to meet family expectations, for example, can be problematic for the family and can sometimes be job-killing for senior executives. The key is to understand the family's self-interests and to make sure they know what to expect. It also helps—a lot—if their expectations are realistic. As it is not uncommon for the self-interest of some family members to be quixotic, it then becomes your responsibility to help ground the family members in reality.

We will discuss in greater detail how to gain a better understanding of family members' self-interests (see Chapter 5). Here we want to give you a 5-step process that you can use to build a high-performing single-family office (Exhibit 3.1):

EXHIBIT 3.1: Help the Family Achieve Its Self-Interests

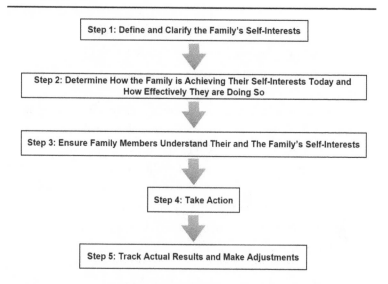

Step 1: Define and Clarify the Family's Self-Interests

Step 2: Determine How the Family is Achieving Their Self-Interests Today and How Effectively They are Doing So

Step 3: Ensure Family Members Understand Their and The Family's Self-Interests

Step 4: Take Action

Step 5: Track Actual Results and Make Adjustments

Step 1: Define and clarify the family's self-interests: You need to discover the self-interest of family members concerning their single-family office. This always entails determining their expectations when it comes to the overall aim of the single-family office as well as the desired outcomes of specific services and products.

An easy example is investment management. When it comes to the monies managed by the single-family office as a whole and all the particular investments therein, projections are the norm. Although various factors such as risk tolerance and time frames are instrumental in constructing the investment portfolio and selecting investments, the family is probably looking for a certain return on their investments. You must be acutely aware of that expectation.

Other services, such as bill paying and tax preparation for example, are similar to investment management. It is easy to ascertain the family's expectations. When it comes to bill paying, timing and accuracy are usually the critical factors. Bills need to be paid when due (or when the family says so) and precision is a must. Tax preparations need to be done timely and flawlessly.

It can sometimes be a little more difficult to ascertain the self-interests of family members when it comes to wealth planning and lifestyle services. This does not mean they do not have strong expectations, but uncovering them can sometimes be a little more complicated. You might have to dig a little and probe until you understand the logic the family members are using as well as the emotional issues.

When the senior generation does estate planning, for instance, they know what they want to happen. Most of the time, the tools and techniques and the structures and strategies used can be alien to them. But they know the outcomes they want. You need to know their self-interests. You want to understand what they want to achieve—the big picture and all the tactical considerations.

Many families are interested in concierge medicine. Simply

put, they want top-quality healthcare—the big picture. This is their overarching self-interest. By digging deeper, you might find the family wants:

- Quick access to a physician for timely diagnosis and immediate treatment

- The ability to obtain a second opinion to verify a diagnosis or treatment plan or to get a different perspective

- Having a qualified physician who oversees treatment across specialists

- Physicians with the ability to monitor a family member's health long-distance

Going deeper is necessary to get at the self-interests of family members. All of this centers on the human element, which we discuss in Chapter 5.

Step 2: Determine how the family is achieving their self-interests today and how effectively they are doing so: With or without a single-family office, successful families are taking steps to get the results they want. Lacking a single-family office, they are probably using various professionals from private bankers to lawyers to accountants to wealth managers. Commonly, the inability of these professionals to capably coordinate is a factor in successful families opting to establish a single-family office.

You need to know what the family is presently doing. Some of the issues are:

- Which professionals is the family relying on?

- How do they choose who to work with?

- How are they measuring the effectiveness of these different professionals?

- What kind of results are they getting?

- What is the biggest stumbling block or problems they are having with each professional?

If they have a single-family office, these same concerns are present. More specifically:

- How effective is their single-family office?

- How are they judging the efficacy of their single-family office?

- What issues are they having with their single-family office?

- Where are the problems originating?

- What actions have been taken to mitigate these complications?

You may very well find that the family is not getting superior results—whether they have a single-family office or not. A likely part of the problem is that they are working with professionals that are just not that good. Another possibility when they are indeed working with high-caliber professionals is a lack of coordination among the experts. All the different professionals are concentrating on what they can do well, consequently losing sight of what might be best for the family.

A very pervasive reason for the family not getting superior results—with or without a single-family office—is the failure of the advisors to deeply understand and focus on the self-interests of family members. This can regularly be seen when the family members themselves are unable to clearly articulate their self-interests. Making sure they do is, therefore, your responsibility.

Step 3: Ensure family members understand their own and the family's self-interests: Often, the biggest complication holding back a single-family office from becoming high-performing is confusion over expectations. Simply put, the family has self-interests that went unfulfilled. Even when expectations are met, they had somehow morphed so that the single-family office under-performed.

A lot of these problems are communication-based. The "I thought you meant" line becomes very popular when results, let alone superior results, are not there. Presumptions of family members and senior executives that are not verified can also easily get the single-family office off course.

A major complication is family members with differing self-interests. So far, we have mostly talked about the family's self-interests. This is only a good way of thinking about the single-family office when there is a sole family decision-maker. When the single-family office is an autocracy, it can be easier for you as a senior executive to know what is expected.

Most single-family offices have multiple family members involved—sometimes directly and sometimes unobtrusively—in major decisions. It is more the norm than not, for different family members to have self-interests that not only do not align but conflict.

To avoid all the ways the family and senior management can conflict because of misunderstandings, the expectations for the single-family office writ large and the expectations for the different services and products are specified and set out, and formally agreed to.

As we said, everyone is well-served when everyone involved

believes the expectations are tied to reality. What occasionally comes out of this process is the need to reel in some family members whose expectations are a little out there. The following are some examples where there was a need to help family members temper their expectations:

- A risk-free investment return of 20% year in and year out

- Protecting assets from unfounded lawsuits and the like while maintaining total control over the assets

- Eliminating income and other taxes by using multiple interconnected legal structures in different jurisdictions all controlled by the same person

At any point in time, it might be necessary for you to make sure all parties are on the same page. Taking this approach makes certain what is not likely or is completely unrealistic is dealt with, thereby avoiding serious problems later on. Helping family members be realistic is essential for you to do your job well.

Step 4: Take action: Put another way: Do the job! If you are responsible for managing the money, you need to invest it well. If you are responsible for estate planning, you will probably use strategies that mitigate taxes. Unfortunately, to the surprise and chagrin of many professionals, doing the job as well as possible can miss the mark because of the differing self-interests of family members.

A great many inner-circle single-family office senior executives skip the previous three steps and start here. Then a good percentage are dumbfounded when the family is not happy with the results they produced. Many single-family office senior executives run into problems because they fail to recognize that delivering superior results is only possible when they understand family member expectations. Investing family money and beating the indices by 15%—objectively—is considered a superior result, unless the family anticipated you will beat the indices by 25%.

Yes, you must do the best job you possibly can. At the same time, you must frame the results you achieve in accord with the self-interests of the family. Let us conclude that you are very talented and capable in your field. Let us also conclude that you need to make the family recognize the value you are delivering. Sometimes the value you provide is evident. Often, it is not and therefore it is up to you to connect the dots for the family.

Always remember, as an inner-circle senior executive in the single-family office, you are responsible for delivering superior results. What those solutions are depends on the services and products involved and what the family expects.

Step 5: Track actual results and make adjustments, including addressing the disparities between outcomes and family self-interests: Anticipation of superior results are nice. Actual superior results are much better. You always want to be tracking actual results and matching them up to the family's self-interests.

Tracking results is powerful and key to building a high-performing single-family office. Doing so . . .

- Let's you help family members refine their expectations and steer clear of surprises as circumstances change;

- Enables you to make adjustments and improvements from getting better external experts to educating family members on how to make the best use of their single-family office;

- And is often essential as a way to demonstrate the value you provide to the family.

In high-performing single-family offices, most—occasionally all—of the different services and products provided to the family are tracked with the aim of constant improvement. However, this is presently not the case in a large percentage of single-family offices, which is why stress testing is so prevalent (see Chapter 7).

Conclusion

Simply put:

- A high-performing single-family office delivers on the family office promise—superior results
- Superior results are outcomes that enable family members to achieve their self-interests, including meeting or exceeding their expectations.

We gave you a 5-step process to help you think through what you need to do to build a high-performing single-family office. By going through each step—without making presumptions— you are more likely to understand what it is going to take to get superior results.

For this all to happen, you must concentrate your efforts on the family. In the single-family office industry, the mantra is *family first*. We explain what this means and your role in the next chapter.

CHAPTER 4

The Meaning of Family First

SINGLE-FAMILY OFFICES ARE about control and gaining significantly greater advantages in life. High-performing single-family offices make good on the family office promise by delivering superior results. They do this by generating enormous value through intense attention to the human element, a top-of-the-line cohesive team, and by being systematic (see next section).

What we have repeatedly found is that a large percentage of single-family offices are not high-performing, and many of them will likely never be high-performing. Even those single-family offices who engage the most talented and brilliant professionals are unlikely to ever be categorized as high-performing. Actually, it can be *because* they engaged the most talented and brilliant professionals.

The Nature of Expertise

What matters more? Is it you or your team's technical abilities, such as investment expertise or wealth planning proficiencies, or your ability to connect on a deep level with family members, other professionals, and your teammates?

Take a moment to carefully consider your answer.

Actually, you need both. Technical expertise and the ability to build rapport are extremely important and essential to building a high-performing single-family office. To be clear . . . single-family offices cannot be high-performing unless both are present.

In studying all types of family offices as well as all types of leading professionals such as wealth managers, accountants, attorneys, private bankers, and so forth, we have discovered the emphasis is very, very often heavily weighted to the technical side. That does not mean many of the single-family office senior executives or the professionals are not adept at establishing and enhancing business relationships, but doing so is given much less emphasis compared to being proficient with the mechanics of the services and products family offices provide.

Let us take for granted that you and the experts you work with are exceptionally technically capable. As we just said, this is a requirement in order to have a high-performing single-family office. The complication is that most of the very best experts are actually fungible.

Technical expertise is increasingly commoditized: Reality check: there are no *exclusive* legal, financial, administrative, or lifestyle solutions. There is nothing available that is inherently unique.

In principle, an exceptional wealth planner can conceivably use all the same tools and techniques as another exceptional wealth planner. Investment management is also more and more a commodity at the high-end. This holds true for administrative and lifestyle services as well.

This DOES NOT mean that all professionals are just as competent. Without question, that is *not* the case. At the top of each profession, there are experts who are exceptionally good at what they do. Among these cohorts, the ability to interchange the professionals and get exceptional results is often good. This is not always the case, but it can happen. Thus, most of them are fungible. Keep in mind, we are talking about the very top of the professions. Those professionals who have reached this level of proficiency are very different—and very much better—than their peers who are not at this level.

We will say that your own expertise and your ability to have these exceptional professionals on your cohesive team is a given. However, having all this talent working with you on behalf of the family does not necessarily produce a high-performing single-family office. As we just noted, it can possibly work against having a high-performing single-family office.

Family, Family, Family

Ironically, the biggest obstacle to building a high-performing single-**family** office is not making it all about the family. Look at most conferences for single-family offices. The agenda is replete with presentations and discussions of technical issues from investment strategies to immigration law to international tax mitigation strategies to cyber-security. There are also sessions on governance and selling companies. Basically, most—not all—single-family office events fail to address what matters most—being attuned to the family.

This DOES NOT mean that technical issues are not important. They are very, very important. It is just that getting requisite expertise that will produce superior results is rarely an obstacle.

Let us put it this way . . . there is no expertise that we cannot source for a successful family. There is no magic here. That means that conceivably there is no expertise that you cannot source for a successful family. It is all about having a deep network of professions and other providers.

If we do not know a high-caliber professional that the family needs, we certainly know someone who does. It is never more than three degrees of separation.

What, then how: In the private wealth industry, and we are including a large number of single-family offices, the emphasis is mistakenly almost exclusively on technical proficiencies. Again, making sure you can provide the family with the highest level of expertise is absolutely critical.

Just as important—and many times more valuable—is truly understanding the self-interests of the family members. When you truly understand **what** the family wants to accomplish and you have a cohesive team composed of the finest experts, you have both the **what** and the **how**. All too often, many professionals do not really understand the family's self-interests because they are too wrapped up in how.

Without intense attention to the self-interests of the family, all their technical wizardry is not going to produce a high-performing single-family office. We were once called in to see what could be done about a single-family office that was about to implode, complete with family members suing each other and worse (much worse). Besides engaging some of the smartest external experts around, the single-family office housed some technical savants of their own.

The investment performance of this single-family office easily beat their designated benchmarks for years. The multi-jurisdictional tax planning they did was subtly elegant and ingenious, helping the family save a tremendous amount of money. These conclusions were based on our outside assessment of the situation.

The problem was that the family members had different and sometimes wilder expectations. In effect, they were disappointed, unhappy, and in some cases, furious about the results they were getting and the way their single-family office was operating. The conclusion was the dissolution of the single-family office with the family members taking their chips and each going off on their own. So, even with what might be classified as objective superior results, this was not a high-performing single-family office. It ended up not being a single-family office at all.

Your Role in the High-Performing Single-Family Office

As a senior executive and part of the inner circle at the single-family office, the technical knowledge and skills you bring are indeed valuable. But just as valuable is your ability to deeply understand the people you are dealing with and your ability to find ways to help them succeed.

This is very much the case when it comes to the family. A high-performing single-family office delivers superior results as defined by the family. To be precise . . .

> *The high-performing single-family office is
> ALL about the family.*

To build a high-performing single-family office, you—as an inner-circle senior executive—help ensure that family members achieve their self-interests with the caveats we previously noted. Yes, based on your personal areas of expertise, you will often be involved in dealing with the mechanics of products and services. But, being attuned to what really matters to family members and what does not puts you into an entirely different league than the majority of professionals.

Your self-interests: While we have strongly emphasized concentrating on the self-interests of the family, before you can do that well, you will need to clearly and precisely understand your self-interests. While we say the single-family office is all about the family, it is just as much about you, and that is where you have to start and end.

There is, for example, a limit to what you can do and what you might want to do. One family looked at their single-family office staff as something akin to indentured servants. The staff was always on call to address any whim. We do mean any whim, exemplified by:

- Bringing aspirin to the family's second estate at 3 AM, which was an hour drive away, because a family member had a headache, even though there was over-the-counter pain medication already at the house. When the senior executive arrived, the family member had already gone to sleep and verbally assaulted the senior executive for waking him up.

- Being unexpectedly instructed to care for the grandchildren (under the age of 10) because of an unplanned whim to go shopping. Meanwhile, the senior executive's daughter's wedding overlapped this request.

- Being responsible for reeling in the spending of some spendthrift heirs. When the senior executives suggested closing down their access to funds, they were screamed at for being insensitive and stifling.

Now, if the compensation working at this single-family office was considered appropriate to deal with these and similar issues on top of doing their official jobs, then catering to the family members might be acceptable. In these examples, the requests of the family could be diplomatically referred to as scope creep.

Working for successful families can be a complete joy and can sometimes be a living hell. We conclude that working for successful families is usually somewhere in between these two extremes, leaning to the complete joy. You have your own agenda and it has to align with that of the family's for the arrangement to be productive and for all parties to feel good about it.

When you are not achieving your self-interests, you can become frustrated, angry, and even bitter. This does you no good. It also proves detrimental to the single-family office and to the ongoing success of the family.

When You Are Family and When You Are Not

The single-family office exists for the shared benefit of the family. Your dual roles—being a family member and a senior executive—can often prove complicated.

Consider the executive director of a single-family office controlling billions of dollars. He was asked by his parents to help them find the right physicians and medical care for some non-life-threatening medical issues. If this situation involved other family members, he would assign the project to one of his staff. Also, the way the single-family office is set up, there would be a cost to the family members for assisting them.

The complication is that his parents wanted him to be directly involved. If he is going to be directly involved, does he have the single-family office charge them? Distilling the matter down . . . what does he do, and is he acting as their son or the head of the single-family office?

Situations like this one are pretty common when family members are part of senior management. Then the issue is . . .

Where do familial responsibilities begin and end?

As more family members want to be included in decision-making positions within single-family offices, conflicts of interest are only going to multiply.

Family dynamics, such as who you deeply care about and to whom you are loyal to, can also impact the functioning of your single-family office. You might very well make exceptions for certain family members and not for other ones. Your family history can also affect how the single-family office runs.

In one family we worked with, decisions were always colored by an ongoing conflict between the founder's two children. Just about all discussions, from where to invest the family fortune to who would be given loans from the family bank, seemed to digress into a reenactment of a few holiday dinners that ended up in fistfights—and, one time, one of the siblings accidentally fired off a shotgun.

Being a family member and an inner-circle senior executive at your single-family office often entails being able to separate your roles. When are you family and when are you the senior executive? This can be tricky.

When you are not a family member but there are senior executives that are family members: Having family members as part of senior management can be helpful if they can provide insights to the self-interests of other family members. It can be positive for the single-family office, and conceivably for you, if they have the knowledge and skills for the roles they have.

In one situation, because of ongoing family businesses and the vast amounts of money involved, a single-family office had established several committees where issues were considered and decisions were occasionally made. Talking a lot and having many, many seemingly never-ending meetings without coming to any decision was the norm, to the disappointment of most of the family.

A second-generation family member became part of senior management. She became critical in moving projects forward. Being smart, humble, and concerned for the welfare of her family led her to circumvent the committees and build consensus among key family members. The end result was a single-family office delivering what the family wanted.

On the other hand, family members who are there to stroke their egos or are involved out of default can be deleterious to the success of the single-family office. If the family members are using their positions to better themselves irrespective of the family's self-interests or are woefully out of their depth yet have the authority to make (bad) decisions, all involved will likely suffer.

One family member, for example, was put on the board of the single-family office. He did graduate from a prestigious business school but lacked any real-world experience. He was always certain of the best way to deal with any situation and was incredibly confident in his investment prowess (he did finish third in the investment simulation contest at the business school). Within about six months of joining the single-family office, he was put in charge of the investment committee. In a little less than two years, the single-family office's investment portfolio was 20% below their benchmarks. It was at this time that the family gently pushed him out of the single-family office.

When unprepared, incompetent, or Machiavellian family members are given authority in the single-family office, you have to be on your guard. By and large, it can take a while before these family members make things so bad that the family moves them out of their roles.

In all cases, always remember . . .

Family is blood, and you are the hired help.

Conclusion

Being adept at understanding the self-interests of family members as well as other professionals and providers combined with technical brilliance will produce a high-performing single-family office. The highest levels of technical expertise are—and will always be—essential to have a high-performing single-family office. Relatively speaking, obtaining that expertise is easy. The hard part is helping the family achieve their self-interests.

At the same time, you have to be cognizant of your self-interests. You want to make sure the arrangement you have with the single-family office is mutually beneficial. Both sides have to consider it fair—or, at least, fair enough.

In the next section, we will look at all three of the core characteristics of high-performing single-family offices. We will start with the human element by showing how the Everyone Wins Process lets you address the question of discerning people's self-interests.

PART II

Core Characteristics of High-Performing Single-Family Offices

CHAPTER 5

The Human Element

A S WE DISCUSSED, a large percentage of financial, legal, and other professionals are highly focused on their specific area of expertise. It is as if they have tunnel vision. If they manage money, for example, their thinking revolves around how they can get better returns—and that might very well be all they think about when it comes to the single-family office or the family. This might be good if managing money is exclusively why you are hiring the professional. But it is unlikely to be good if this is you—an inner-circle single-family office senior executive.

High-performing single-family offices can address a broad array of a successful family's needs, wants, and concerns. Even if you are product-oriented, because you are part of the single-family office inner circle, you must be concerned with investment performance as it relates to the expectations of the family. You must be focused on the human element.

Without question, the human element is the foundational ingredient in your ability to attain superior results for the family. While there might be cultural differences that enhance and optimize business relationships, the human element is instrumental in building a high-performing single-family office. The human element is predicted in the Everyone Wins Process.

The Everyone Wins Process

For the sake of full transparency, there is no magic, no secrets to the Everyone Wins Process. You are more than likely already doing many of the things we will be advocating. The big difference between what you are doing and what we are advocating is probably the extent you think about it and how methodical you are. We repeatedly find that few single-family office senior executives or professionals, or just about anyone else for that matter, are thoughtful and methodical.

Before going into the components and practices of the Everyone Wins Process, there are a couple of underlying concepts you need to be cognizant of:

People behave in accordance with their self-interests.

People are not going to do what you want them to. They are going to do what *they* want to do. To achieve your agenda, you first have to help them achieve *their* agendas. By helping family members achieve their self-interests, you are able to better achieve your own self-interests. This also holds for the professionals and providers you engage on behalf of the single-family offices (see next chapter).

Another underlying concept . . .

You need to make a very large percentage of your conversations and actions all about them and their self-interests.

By making it all about them, you further uncover their self-interests, letting you know how you can help them achieve their agendas. Only by deeply understanding the self-interests of family members are you able to know how the single-family office can help them pursue their hopes and dreams as well as best deal with their concerns and worries.

This perspective is essential to building a high-performing single-family office. By helping family members achieve their self-interests, you are best positioned to be highly compensated (see Chapter 8). The bottom line ... everyone wins.

The Everyone Wins Process, for instance, is essential in all forms of personal wealth creation coaching, discussed in Appendix B. The Everyone Wins Process consists of four main steps (see Exhibit 5.1).

EXHIBIT 5.1: The Everyone Wins Process

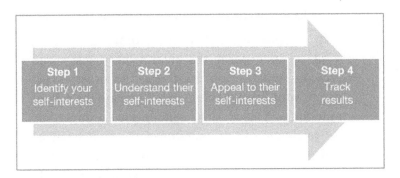

Step 1	Step 2	Step 3	Step 4
Identify your self-interests	Understand their self-interests	Appeal to their self-interests	Track results

Source: Everyone Wins! How You Can Enhance and Optimize Business Relationships Just Like Ultra-Wealthy Entrepreneurs

Step 1: Your self-interests: As we talked about in the previous chapter, while you are intent on helping other people, ranging from family members to other professionals and providers engaged by the single-family office, achieve their self-interests, you have to also achieve your self-interests. Only then does everyone win. Therefore, you start by determining your self-interests, such as your most important goals, issues, and concerns.

Let us say your self-interests include becoming personally wealthy. It is therefore useful to know what you want to be worth. Let us refer to this number as your financial end-goal. Now, to reach your financial end-goal, you will need to take several smaller steps along the way. The following three steps can help you lay out the path—broadly speaking—to your financial end-goal . . .

- **Step 1: State your financial end-goal:** Decide on the number you are aiming for. It should be reasonable. Idealistic objectives are well and good, but at the moment, you need to be singularly interested in money and you have to be somewhat realistic.

- **Step 2: Identify critical milestones:** You then need to brainstorm the intermediary goals and accomplishments you must reach in order to get you to your financial end-goal. These are the critical milestones. You must be able to draw a direct line between your critical milestones and your financial end-goal. You need to specify how being an inner-circle single-family office senior executive will help you reach your financial end-goal. You want to think about the compensation and the relationships you will establish because of your position.

- **Step 3: Always be aware of your financial end-goal and critical milestones:** All too often, people lose sight of their goals and objectives. Their attention wanes. You need to stay focused and not let yourself get sidetracked. Simply put, you cannot lose sight of your own self-interests.

There are two ways to think about self-interests—strategic and tactical. You need to know what success means to you. You have to specify the big picture outcomes you want. These are referred to as your strategic self-interests.

When it comes to your role in the single-family office, your self-interests probably involve your compensation. It also will probably deal with opportunities for advancement and the responsibilities you have at the single-family office. It might involve the professional network you can build among the financial elite and their providers. Put another way, these are your financial end-goal and critical milestones.

You also have an ongoing and often expanding plethora of tactical self-interests. Every time you communicate with someone, there is usually some way you can move your self-interests forward. From negotiating fee structures with a provider to the single-family office to educating family members on an investment, you have tactical self-interests you want to attain. With the Everyone Wins Process, a perpetual tactical self-interest is to further uncover the self-interests of others. Remember to keep your agenda in your mind in all your business interactions.

Being constantly cognizant of your self-interests enhances your competency and your ability to achieve your goals. Moreover, by being clear about your self-interests, you can put all your energy into determining the other person's self-interests.

Step 2: Their self-interests: Developing a deep understanding of family members and other professionals and providers you are working with is indispensable to building a high-performing single-family office. It is amazingly easy to get surface information about someone else. Surface information, however, is not enough. To effectively enhance, and possibly optimize, business relationships requires a deep understanding, as opposed to surface understanding.

Determining what is important as well as what is not important to family members can sometimes be challenging. While there are obvious self-interests that can easily tie to products and services such as solid investment performance, for instance—the opaque and carefully hidden self-interests are often what truly drive people.

Family dynamics can cause a shift in self-interests fairly quickly, making your job confusing and more difficult. Think about the scenario where a single-family office senior executive was doing an amazing job of managing a portion of the family's investment portfolio. Objectively, it was in the interest of the family to have him continue managing money. He was, however, quickly replaced by the new fiancée of a family member. He was still involved in selecting investments, which lasted until his job search resulted in a new position. Incidentally, after a few years, the new family member by marriage was expelled from the single-family office.

Determining the self-interests of external experts and other providers is considerably easier. Still, do not make the mistake of being presumptuous. Yes, they want to work with the single-family office to generate revenues. But these people have other self-interests tied to their business. By learning about these other self-interests, you will be better able to arrive at more favorable arrangements for your single-family office (see next chapter).

We have found that many external experts want to work with single-family offices for the prestige and validation of their knowledge and abilities. When we have been able to help these external experts constructively capitalize on the association, they were willing to charge less for their expertise or deliver more for their stated fees.

Central to ascertaining the self-interests of other people is the discovery process. The discovery process artfully uses open-ended questions and probes to uncover the self-interests of others. Examples of powerful discovery questions include:

- What is the most important thing we should be discussing?
- What are you most concerned about?
- What do you think?
- What do you see as the best and worst outcomes?
- Can you tell me more?

At the core of the discovery process is adopting a curiosity mindset. Curiosity connects to all aspects of human advancement. It is the fundamental psychological concept behind learning. Being curious means you are sincerely interested in the lives of other people in a very broad way. Curiosity lets you move far beyond using checklists, decision trees, or scripts. It enables you to immerse yourself in discovering what makes someone tick.

Discovery is about learning the thoughts, ideas, beliefs, and so forth of other people. Frankly, it is very hard to do that when you are talking. We, therefore, recommend you follow the

10% Rule. You do not talk more than 10% of the time during a conversation if you intend to ascertain the other person's self-interests.

But there is another step here that you must take. It involves the use of empathy and empathetic listening skills to confirm you truly understand the other person and you have identified information that will be useful in helping everyone win. When you use empathetic statements and responses, you can determine whether you have accurately heard and interpreted information from others. Think of your empathetic responses as trial balloons. They are ways of confirming whether you are on the right track. Empathy helps reduce errors and misperceptions in business relationships.

Additionally, empathetic responses tell people you not only understand but also care—which in turn further motivates them to open up to you and reveal even more information that may help you identify their self-interests. Empathy is intertwined with discovery. It is how you confirm your understanding of their self-interest as well as let them know you understand.

Step 3: Appeal to their self-interests: Knowing your self-interest strategically and tactically and their self-interests permits you to help them achieve their agenda and your agenda. It also lets you effectively move forward to get results.

With your success, as defined by your compensation and potential for advancement, for example, being tied to the success of the single-family office, your ability to align the two sets of self-interests is crucial. When this happens, you have *enlightened self-interests* (Exhibit 5.2).

EXHIBIT 5.2: Enlightened Self-Interests

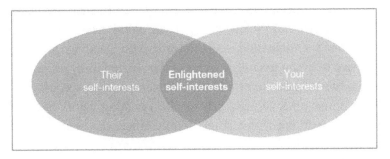

Source: Everyone Wins! How You Can Enhance and Optimize Business Relationships Just Like Ultra-Wealthy Entrepreneurs

Many times, to reach a state of enlightened self-interests, you have to move beyond the obvious. For instance, great investment performance is likely a goal of the family and the investment professionals working for the single-family office. But there are times when the self-interests involved include more than just great investment performance. It is not uncommon for egos to be tightly enmeshed when investment strategies are working well. When this is the case, you may need to reinforce the self-image of particular people in order to maintain the success you are getting.

When the single-family office is a benevolent dictatorship, the decision-maker is evident. However, the way decisions are made in many single-family offices involves multiple people, each with their own self-interests. Understanding who has the most influence and how to generate broader alignment becomes very important.

With each person, find what matters most to them and show them how their self-interests align with the family's overall agenda. Doing so is a factor in building a high-performing single-family office. The ability to help build consensus among family members plays a big part in getting things done.

When working with external experts and other providers to the single-family office, you will again need to pursue everyone's enlightened self-interests. You need to find the overlap between the self-interest of the single-family office and the professionals and providers. For example, the psychological high some professionals get, or the bragging rights because they are working with a single-family office, can be important to these people. If this is the case, you want to make it a part of the relationship.

It is essential to recognize that appealing to someone's self-interest is NOT about persuasion or influence. You are identifying ways you can sincerely and meaningfully add value. You are determining the opportunities and possibilities that exist in order to bring people together. It is about making determined efforts to help other people accomplish their objectives and mitigate their concerns—to achieve their self-interests (and your self-interests).

Step 4: Track results: In the previous chapter, we recommended you address the self-interests of the family. Part of that process is to determine their expectations and track how they match up with what actually happens. This gives you the opportunity to adjust and refine family members' expectations presently and in the future.

Along the same lines, it is always worthwhile to track the results of the decisions and the actions that are taken. By tracking results in real-time, you can avoid possible explosions down the line. For instance, you do not want family members to be unhappy with a service, but you only find this out when they are very unhappy, and the consequences are much worse.

Because you are tracking results constantly, you are able to make necessary adjustments and refinements before family members become upset about what is going on.

When tracking results with external experts and other providers, you are looking to evaluate how their arrangements with the single-family office are working for them. Not for the single-family office, but specifically for them. In order for the single-family office to get preferential arrangements from external experts and other providers, they have to see meaningful benefits for themselves. Knowing their self-interests lets you deliver and show them value beyond the fees the single-family office is paying.

Consider a law firm not only making money doing work for the single-family office but also, with the help of inner-circle single-family office senior executives, was able to land some significant new clients. These were not other family offices, but substantial high-net-worth clients. The senior executives tracked the results in terms of the number of new high-net-worth clients, but—more importantly—the revenues these clients generated. This information proved very useful when the single-family office negotiated with the law firm for additional work. The senior executives were able to get the same quality legal advice at a lower hourly rate.

When using the Everyone Wins Process, by being aware of how things are going, you can markedly accelerate your success. Unless you are tracking results, you do not know if you are helping the family or other professionals achieve their self-interests. At the same time, you need to know if your efforts are going to get you the results you are looking for.

Just like the single-family office was able to lower the fees of the law firm because it was instrumental in getting them additional high-net-worth clients, you can improve your standing at the single-family office because of the value you have brought. As your value is not always self-evident, you may need to be able to point to specific examples and situations—thus the need for tracking.

Taking Action

Central to building a high-performing single-family office is the need to understand and address the self-interests of family members and external experts. In the private wealth industry, this is often referred to as *the human element*.

The self-interests of the family members encompass their expectations concerning their single-family office, but goes much further. It also includes several considerations. With respect to each family member, aspects of their self-interests might include . . .

- What they want from their single-family office and how it fits into the rest of their lives
- What they want to personally accomplish—goals, wishes, and dreams
- What keeps them up at night—concerns, anxieties, and fears
- What they are looking for from their different personal and professional relationships, including what they expect from you
- Their underlying rationale for their wants, concerns, and expectations
- How they see themselves—their self-image
- The information they are using that supports their strongly held beliefs

Upon the self-interests of individual family members, you build a high-performing single-family office. You know what matters to them and, just as importantly, what does not matter. You will know how they define value, thereby enabling you to work within their worldview. You know what they expect from their single-family office and from you.

Being proficient at ascertaining a family member's—or any person's—self-interests is not always easy. Aside from know-how, determining the self-interests of others can take a concerted effort. Moreover, even when you are good at eliciting the self-interests of family members, you can still further refine your skills.

As an experiment . . .

For three family members, can you identify the three most important issues for each of them outside of their health and the health of loved ones?

When we ask this question of both family and non-family inner-circle senior executives at single-family offices, we more likely than not find two outcomes. Either the senior executives do not know with any degree of certainty or they are wrong on at least one, and more likely two, of a family member's most important issues.

As we have discussed, family members are not the only people whose self-interests you should be aware of. To get superior business (and often personal) results, knowing a person's self-interests is crucial. Knowing the self-interests of other senior executives and staff at the single-family office, as well as the self-interest of all the professionals and providers involved, is also very powerful.

Conclusion

The human element is essential to building a high-performing single-family office. This in no way minimizes the importance of top-of-the-line technical capabilities. It is just that most times, throughout the private wealth industry, technical capabilities are mistakenly seen as singularly important. However, without the human element, even the most erudite experts in the world may never get the chance to properly apply their brilliance.

Conceptually, the Everyone Wins Process is universal. It has been validated over thousands of years. However, when implementing the process, cultural differences are evident. How to best ask questions—tone, manner, approach, and so forth—can vary considerably throughout the world. Therefore, you have to adapt the Everyone Wins Process to your culture. You will also need to adapt the Everyone Wins Process to your personality and the way you are comfortable and effective in working with others.

One of the most constructive ways to become more attuned to other people's self-interests is to master the Everyone Wins Process. You not only know their self-interests, you are also making certain their self-interests are part of many—possibly all—of the conversations you have with them. For instance, you will regularly tie back your actions and decisions to their self-interests. When it comes to external experts and providers, the approach pays great dividends. We will discuss how in the following chapter.

If you want to learn more about the Everyone Wins Process, the book—*Everyone Wins! How You Can Enhance and Optimize Business Relationships Just Like Wealthy Entrepreneurs*—is available on Amazon.

CHAPTER 6

A Cohesive Team

To get superior results—to build a high-performing single-family office—you need a cohesive team. Without question, there is no way to deliver the array of expertise that a single-family office can conceivably deliver without a solid team of internal and external talented professionals.

What is important to understand is that we are talking about a well-coordinated, well-functioning, supportive team—*a cohesive team*. While many single-family offices make extensive use of external experts, this does not mean they have a cohesive team. It is common for these external experts to be brought in and operate mostly independently. This is not the way to get superior results.

High-performing family office senior executives recognize their strengths and weaknesses. They buffer their limitations by working with and coordinating extremely capable specialists inside and outside the single-family office. All together, they form the cohesive team necessary for superior results. Keep in mind that your cohesive team is built around the successful family—what it wants; what it needs. Therefore, the cohesive team must be able to readily adapt to changes in the family's world.

Three Key Attributes of a Cohesive Team

You need to make sure the team works efficiently and effectively. That means the cohesive team must consistently deliver excellence. A high-performing single-family office only exists if the team works in a synchronized manner and is laser-focused to help the family in ways that matter.

It is important to note that we are not just talking about a team. We are intentionally including the word *cohesive* to describe the team. With a cohesive team, for example, there are no handoffs to specialists. As an inner-circle single-family office senior executive, you or another person in a similar position is always either directly involved or overseeing what is going on and keeping everything on track.

There are many attributes of a cohesive team (Exhibit 6.1). We will address three of the more important and sometimes overlooked qualities.

EXHIBIT 6.1: Key Attributes of a Cohesive Team

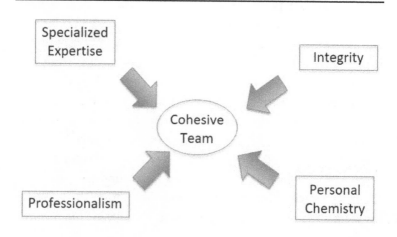

Best of the best: The cohesive team must be composed of some of the most capable and talented experts in investment management, wealth planning, and other fields such as concierge medicine, family security, and personal development. How to find these external experts is discussed below. High-caliber cohesive teams composed of the best of the best have four central characteristics:

- **Specialized knowledge and skills:** The professionals and providers are some of the best in their fields. What matters is that the members of your cohesive team are truly exceptional at what they do.

- **Integrity:** The highest ethical standards are indispensable for all the professionals and providers you work with.

- **Professionalism:** In every way, from responsiveness to inquiries to continuous learning, the members of your cohesive team must embrace professionalism.

- **Personal chemistry:** There should be a strong level of comfort and appreciation among everyone on your cohesive team. Your ability to establish enlightened self-interests is crucial here.

State-of-the-art capabilities: The cohesive team must be able to deliver the appropriate solutions to match the family's requirements, from the most basic to state-of-the-art. What singularly defines state-of-the-art capabilities is that the quality of implementation of the best solutions is always exceptional. This means that execution is:

- **Error-free:** Mistakes—usually unforced errors—are very rare when it comes to high-performing single-family offices.

- **Cost-effective:** The ability to choose the most appropriate solutions and implement exceedingly well while keeping costs down (not cutting corners) is necessary.

- **Expeditious:** Doing things on time or before the deadline is characteristic of high-performing single-family offices.

Preferential arrangements: The cohesive team must provide the family with the most-favored status. This means family members receive complete and rapid access to the highest level of expertise at highly advantageous pricing. Put another way: high-performing single-family offices do more than bring their cohesive teams to a higher level. They also make sure the family is getting a really good deal.

There are two aspects to preferential arrangements:

- **Cost mitigation:** This means that the high-performing single-family office either pays less for the products and services they receive, or they get more for their money.

- **The ability to jump to the head of the line:** Because of the connectedness of the inner-circle single-family office senior executives, family members can regularly be attended to almost immediately.

There are two aspects to filling the ranks of a cohesive team—hiring talent and outsourcing. In Chapter 8, we will discuss how single-family offices select talent. Here we are going to talk about outsourcing.

The Art of Outsourcing

Single-family offices are not self-contained, considering all the expertise they can conceivably provide. While certain professionals are in-house, ALL high-performing single-family offices engage external experts on an as-needed basis. These outsourced capabilities are carefully overseen by the senior management of the single-family office. There are five key considerations employed by high-performing single-family offices when making outsourcing decisions (Exhibit 6.2):

EXHIBIT 6.2: Key Considerations When Outsourcing

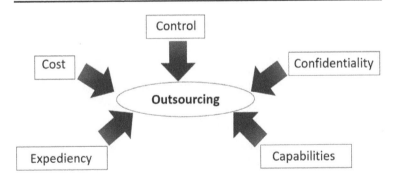

- **Control**: To some degree, all single-family offices are established and maintained because of the family's preference for control. By engaging external experts, a single-family office's influence is lessened. Overall, the **more** control a family wants, the **less** the single-family office will likely outsource.

- **Confidentiality**: Many families work hard to keep their personal lives private. The **more** the family is concerned about privacy, the **less** it will likely outsource. Of course, there is no way to ensure privacy is always maintained. Still, the more the expertise is in-house, the better the ability to limit information leaking out.

- **Cost**: Probably the most powerful driver of regular outsourcing is cost. The **more** cost mitigation is a factor, the **more** the single-family office will likely outsource. There are times, however, when it is more cost-effective to bring certain experts in-house. The ongoing demand for their specialized skills and knowledge is great enough to justify the expense.

- **Capabilities**: Through outsourcing, many single-family offices have greater capabilities. There are constraints on having all the experts in-house. Expense is one, but there are also managerial issues, as well as ensuring that the experts are perpetually at the cutting edge. The **more** the single-family office is tasked with, the **more** it will likely outsource.

- **Expediency**: When there is a pressing need for certain expertise and that expertise is not available in-house, the answer is outsourcing. The **more** that speed is an issue, the **more** likely the single-family office will outsource.

In sum, cost mitigation, increased capabilities, and expediency are driving the trend of single-family offices to outsource. Always being able to have the "best of the best" is often possible only when the single-family office relies on external experts. Also, if something is incredibly time-sensitive, there is a tendency to outsource.

The factors working against single-family office outsourcing are control and confidentiality. If these factors are extremely important, and if the family has the financial resources to bring the "best of the best" in-house, then the single-family office becomes more self-sufficient.

Likelihood of using external experts: All single-family offices outsource. Based on a series of studies over the last decade, we find that single-family offices are more inclined to rely on external experts for certain types of expertise:

- **Investment management** is more likely to be in-house. Asset allocation and rebalancing, for instance, selecting companies to invest in are often done by money managers housed in the single-family office. At the same time, internal experts often select external money managers for specific capabilities.

- **Wealth planning** is usually farmed out to specialists. This ensures the solutions are state-of-the-art. It is regularly a cost-effective approach, as wealth planning expertise is often only required periodically.

- **Administrative services** are generally either in-house or shared. Compliance, however, is habitually outsourced.

- **Lifestyle services and special projects** are almost always dependent on external experts.

When external experts are engaged, high-performing single-family offices always provide guidance and oversight. Nothing is ever just handed off to the specialists.

Sourcing external experts: In finding the best of the best, inner-circle single-family office senior executives use several different approaches. The one they choose to employ at any one time is predicated on circumstances. In order of viability, the following are the approaches used to source external experts:

- **Referrals from other professionals:** Going to leading industry authorities is the predominant way inner-circle single-family office senior executives source many of the external experts they employ. Obtaining referrals from professionals in whom they are very confident is an astute risk-reduction approach.

- **Self-initiated research:** More and more inner-circle single-family office senior executives are reaching out to find external experts. This can take a number of forms. Some of the larger single-family offices are using retained intermediaries, in part, for this purpose.

- **Connecting with thought leaders:** Another factor in sourcing external experts is that the experts tend to be well known among other professionals in the private wealth industry, including their peers. These experts are *thought leaders*. Their willingness to share their knowledge contributes to powerful and influential professional brands that draw the wealthy and other leading authorities to them. More on this in Chapter 8.

- **Referrals from peers**: Around the world, this approach is not that common. Nevertheless, many inner-circle senior executives at different single-family offices are making great efforts to learn best practices from each other. This sets the stage for making referrals to external experts.

- **Previous experience with the external experts**: Inner-circle senior executives at single-family offices are generally wise from experience. They have usually built connections with various professionals they know and trust. They call on these relationships when appropriate.

Sometimes, there is a need for experts that are less commonly called upon by successful families. The high-performing single-family office can source these super-niche specialists.

Super-niche specialists: While no services or products are truly unique or 100% exclusive in the private wealth industry, some astoundingly talented and experienced professionals are *only* accessible by other professionals who are "in the know." These experts are arguably some of the best at what they do, and what they do is usually extremely specialized, such as:

- A prodigious musical theorist turned world-class professional poker player and Platinum Life Master bridge player (because he decided to spend his time in other pursuits) turned hedging strategist. She is concentrating on developing hedges for passion investments and geopolitical upheavals.

- A one-time juvenile delinquent (the files are sealed) who is currently considered one of the foremost experts on asset protection planning for multi-jurisdictional successful families. He is credited with helping develop or refine approaches like the "floating island strategy," which works amazingly well but often necessitates the families are billionaires.

- A GO grandmaster who probably has one of the best track records for winning private trusts and estate lawsuits involving certain offshore jurisdictions. He tends to work for the estates but has been known to play all sides.

While most super-niche specialists engaged by single-family offices deal with wealth management, some address family support. For instance, there are some exclusive boutique health care and family security providers. There is a reclamation expert who—through happenstance—ended up being one of the top professionals when it comes to cult extractions. On the lighter side, we have been able to source a cryptozoologist, a cybernetic soothsayer, a quantum matchmaker, and an award-winning dollhouse architect.

Negotiating with external experts: At high-performing single-family offices, just about all arrangements with external experts comes about through negotiations. For instance, rarely are stated fees the fees paid by high-performing single-family offices.

The only serious exception tends to be when there is a great need to act immediately. For instance, if medical specialists are required, negotiating fees usually becomes a non-issue. Another example is when a family faced a security crisis because of credible death threats. Family security specialists were brought in immediately—cost was no object. This proves to be a very wise decision.

Because of your position in the single-family office, you will probably be involved in negotiating with external experts. The following steps may be useful (Exhibit 6.3):

EXHIBIT 6.3: Negotiating with External Experts

Step 1: Understand the External Expert's Business Model

Step 2: Determine Their Self-Interests

Step 3: Develop a Negotiation Strategy

Step 4: Negotiate

Step 5: Track Results and Make Adjustments in the Future

- **Step 1: Understand the external expert's business model**: You are at a considerable advantage when you understand how external experts make money—not only how their firms make money but how they personally make money. This means you know how their business model operates, from how the equity is shared to whether the professional is given origination credit. There are various ways to reach this understanding. The simplest approach is as part of the discovery process.

- **Step 2: Determine their self-interests**: Certainly, being paid is high on their list of self-interests. But, as we discussed in the previous chapter, they have other self-interests as well. Operational arrangements, for example, tend to be a factor. Among many external experts, for instance, there is an ego boost working with single-family offices and successful families. Moreover, the status derived from working with the single-family office can potentially attract other high-net-worth clients. As always, the more you know their self-interests, the more effectively you can negotiate.

- **Step 3: Develop a negotiation strategy**: Based on the self-interest and requirements of the family and the single-family office, your self-interests, the business model, and the self-interests of each external expert, you can develop a strong negotiation strategy. The general objective is to get the external experts to do an exceptional job for the single-family office at the lowest price. Keep in mind that it is in everyone's best interests for all parties to come out of the negotiation as winners.

- **Step 4: Negotiate**: Now you bargain. Here there is a degree of give and take. By using the Everyone Wins

Process, you are able to make sure all parties arrive at a mutually productive arrangement. Your aim is to focus on everyone's enlightened self-interests.

- **Step 5: Track results and make adjustments in the future:** To improve your ability to negotiate, it is useful to see how the arrangement is working or worked out by tracking results. Often, there are lessons to be learned that make you better, and that you will apply in future negotiations.

Being an inner-circle single-family office senior executive, you may very well be called upon to negotiate agreements with external experts. This is a way for you to demonstrate your value to the family, as almost all these professionals and providers will negotiate their fees and the terms of their engagements.

Tracking results is important in many aspects of building a high-performing single-family office. It is also likely to be important in enabling you to achieve your self-interests. Therefore, when you get better deals with external experts, you certainly need to keep track of them. It also helps if you can show family members how your negotiating prowess benefits them.

Let us say you were able to decrease the asset management fee on an investment advisor from 80 basis points to 55 basis points. How you communicate this to the family can make a big difference. You can point out the decrease in the fee in terms of 25 basis points. Additionally, you can also show them value by explaining that on the US $100 million investment, there is a savings of a quarter of a million dollars (US). Frame this conversation based on your understanding of the family members. Being able to have this discussion in different ways is helpful.

Taking Action

There are different ways you can build your cohesive team. We sometimes find, for instance, new inner-circle single-family office senior executives start with much of their team in place because of their previous roles in the private wealth industry. On the other hand, a large percentage of senior executives tend to build their teams randomly. They engage external experts to put out fires, as opposed to being thoughtfully proactive.

To build your cohesive team, you can use the following steps (Exhibit 6.4) . . .

- **Step 1: Identify, based on the family's self-interests, the expertise required by the single-family office:** Here you are not picking particular specialists. You are only specifying the broad categories, such as investment management or concierge medicine or cross-border tax planning, that will be needed to address the family's self-interests. Still, you want to identify, as much as possible, any particulars. So, you start with investment management and then you break that down into specifics, such as private equity, macro hedge funds, and so forth.

- **Step 2: Determine if the expertise should be outsourced:** Using the five key considerations—control, confidentiality, cost, capabilities, and expediencies—decide whether to bring the requisite professionals or providers in-house or not. This is not an all-or-nothing decision, as there are many likely variations as to what should be internal to the single-family office and what should be outsourced.

- **Step 3: Decide how you want the team to operate**: Thinking through the way the team members will work with the single-family office and with each other (when necessary) is all too often taken for granted. Failing to be thoughtful about this tends to lead to conflicts. When the experts are not informed as to how information moves and how each party needs to act, there is a tendency for them to emphasize their own agendas. Of course, circumstances are likely to periodically upend your processes, but getting all parties on the same page is always a good idea.

- **Step 4: Source and screen potential external experts**: The most common way to find specialists for the single-family office is through your network of professionals and providers. However, this does not mean you should not use all avenues open to you. Over time, you want to put together an extensive database of possible resources that you continuously update.

- **Step 5: Finalize the list of potential external experts**: Based on your initial assessments, you will conduct a more formal technical evaluation. This is how you will decide who you prefer to work with. When you connect with the different potential external experts, you want to quickly move beyond their pitch or story and determine if they are good candidates. At this time, your primary aim is to learn about them and their businesses. You want to know their business models and their self-interests.

- **Step 6: Make the decision as to who to preferably work with and negotiate the arrangement**: Based on all your assessments, decide on which prospective professionals and providers to see if an agreement can be reached. You will likely have one or two preferred choices. Even so, having a backup can be useful from a negotiating standpoint, and if the first choice does not live up to expectations. Then, you negotiate an arrangement (see above).

- **Step 7: Formalize the arrangement and track results**: Most single-family offices codify their working agreements to some degree. Occasionally, single-family offices will document everything, including how team members interact. Formalizing the arrangement at some level is a good way to make sure all parties have the same understandings and expectations. And, as always, track results.

EXHIBIT 6.4: Building a Cohesive Team

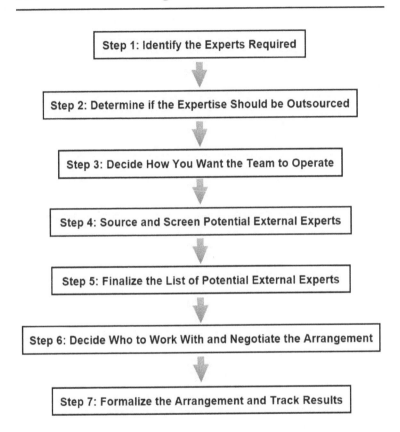

How tightly you need to follow these steps depends on you, other single-family office senior executives, and the family. Even so, it can be useful to address the points in this process to help maximize the value of outsourced relationships.

Conclusion

Today, family offices—whether they are some version of a single-family office or some version of a multi-family office—are not self-contained. It simply does not make economic or business sense. Therefore, you need to bring external experts to the table when appropriate.

To build a high-performing single-family office, you will need to forge a cohesive team. A great cohesive team is one that is replete with top-level professionals and providers who work well together on behalf of the family. What is somewhat ironic is that it can be incredibly difficult to merge brilliant professionals into a team. Thus, you need to skillfully negotiate based on the self-interests of each party as well as the self-interest of the family (and even your own self-interests) to create a cohesive team.

Aside from the intense attention to the human element and a cohesive team, you need systematic processes in order to build a high-performing single-family office—the topic of the next chapter.

CHAPTER 7

Systematic Processes

A COHESIVE TEAM IS indispensable. Outstanding expertise is the only way to get superior results and thus have a high-performing single-family office. Even the most integrated, knowledgeable, and in-tune cohesive team, however, will *not* consistently provide superior results if its approach is muddled or in the least bit chaotic. Getting everyone working harmoniously requires systematic processes.

There are a fair number of systematic processes used by high-performing single-family offices to leverage the power of cohesive teams while concentrating on the human element. Just to emphasize the point: the human element is infused into all systematic processes from the very beginning. For example, in wealth planning, the multitude of legal strategies and financial products are ineffectual if they do not help family members achieve their self-interests. Moreover, by being attentive to the human element, you are best able to explain—at whatever level of detail a family member is comfortable with—what you are recommending, what you are doing, and how the solutions will deliver their desired results.

We are going to look at three systematic processes— investment management, the virtuous cycle used in wealth planning, and stress testing. Because single-family offices are regularly tasked with managing the family's fortune, we will dig deeper into investment management.

Investment Management

When investing to achieve any goal for a single-family office, the investment management process never stops. As investors and generations move through life stages, changes occur—births, divorce, deaths, or shrinking time horizons, which may require adjustments to goals, risk-reward profiles, or asset allocations. As changes occur, or as market or economic conditions dictate, the investment management process begins anew. When we speak of investment management, we are speaking of three categories: goals, processes, and decisions. Single-family offices that bring an open and rational approach to each of these enjoy the fruits of short- and long-term investments.

Part one: high-performing single-family offices use systems thinking: Almost everything is a system. Nature is a system. All biological life cycles are systems. Family is a system. Those single-family offices with the most success in investment management understand the basics of systems thinking.

The term *systems thinking* can mean different things to different people. A good definition is, systems thinking is an understanding and appreciation for the circular nature of the world we live in; an awareness of the role that structure plays in creating the conditions we face; a recognition that powerful laws govern operating systems that we can be unaware of; and a realization that there are consequences to our actions that we can be oblivious to. This approach includes the willingness to see a situation fully, to recognize that we are interrelated, to acknowledge that there are often multiple interventions to a problem, and to champion interventions that may not be popular. Problems that are ideal for systems thinking have the following characteristics:

- The issue is important
- The problem is chronic, not a one-time event
- The problem is familiar and has a known history
- People consistently try to solve the problem successfully

Investment management in any family office satisfies these conditions. The great Benjamin Graham, father of modern investment research and mentor to Warren Buffett, consistently made the point that, "An investment operation is one which, upon thorough analysis, promises safety of principal and an adequate return."

Investment management and systems thinking are not linear. Both happen in cycles, loops, and contours. All parts of the system are connected, so a change in one part generates waves of changes that reach all other parts. Thus, the action returns to the starting point in a modified form—a feedback loop. Our experience is formed as a result of such actions. The phrase *feedback* is often used to designate any reaction, but in reality, it means the perception of the result of our actions affecting subsequent actions (i.e., two-way communication).

Our experience is formed as a result of this kind of feedback loop, although we are used to seeing one-way influence. One example of this in investing comes from the fact that investors are far more distressed by losses than they are delighted by gains. This leads people to discard their winners if they need cash and hold onto their losers because they do not want to recognize or admit that they made a mistake.

Part two: understanding and setting goals: Happiness is a function of expectations. Approaching your goals with intent is critical to success. Often, members of a single-family office have competing goals—different interests—for the investments being made. The cause of these differences lies in what outcomes each is seeking and the best approach to achieving them. When expectations are aligned and met, there is the highest potential for positive results.

We have found that there are four different types of goals many single-family office senior executives can have, which determine how they think about investment management:

- **Preserve**: To create a strategy and family culture that enables wealth to last through multiple generations.

- **Spend**: To support lifestyle goals with the assumption that all wealth will be spent in one's lifetime.

- **Divide**: To identify a set amount of money to either create a minimum wealth level or to leave to beneficiaries.

- **Grow**: To create a strategy and family culture that enables wealth to grow in perpetuity.

Psychology plays a big role in not only setting goals, but sticking with them. Goals are an end state, and the often-stated phrase, "begin with the end in mind," means exactly that. It means you should know where you are going so that you better understand where you are now, and so that the steps you take are always in the right direction.

The biggest psychological problem with many single-family offices when it comes to investment management has to do with time and timing. There is wisdom in knowing that time is the friend to the investor and impulse the enemy. As Vincent Van Gogh said, "Great things do not just happen by impulse, but as a succession of small things linked together."

Investing is not nearly as difficult as it looks. Successful investing involves doing a few things right and avoiding serious mistakes. A partial list of the few things to do right includes having a clear understanding of your goals, managing your emotions, avoiding greed and fear, controlling expenses, properly diversifying your portfolio, maintaining patience and a long-term attitude, knowing where to place your trust, controlling your risk, having a long-term plan, giving up the urge to beat the market, and knowing when to settle for good enough instead of over-reaching.

Part three: the investment process: A good investment process is made up of five distinct steps (Exhibit 7.1).

EXHIBIT 7.1: The Investment Process

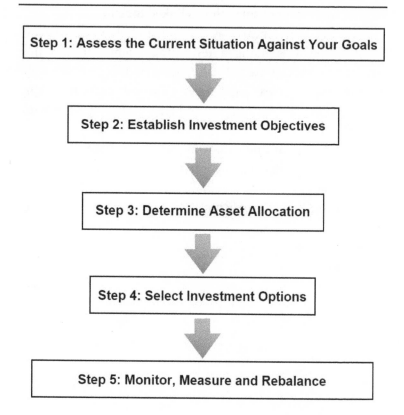

Step 1: Assess the Current Situation Against Your Goals

Step 2: Establish Investment Objectives

Step 3: Determine Asset Allocation

Step 4: Select Investment Options

Step 5: Monitor, Measure and Rebalance

Step 1: assess the current situation against your goals: Planning for the future requires having a clear understanding of the family's current situation in relation to where they want to be. This requires a thorough assessment of current assets, liabilities, cash flow, and investments in light of the family's most important goals. Goals need to be clearly defined and quantified so that the assessment can identify any gaps between the current investment strategy and the stated goals. This step needs to include a frank discussion about the family's values, beliefs, and priorities, all of which set the course for developing an investment strategy.

Step 2: establish investment objectives: There are few things more important and potentially daunting than establishing a long-term investment objective. It centers on identifying the family's risk-return profile. In first-generation single-family offices where there might have been a founder who took outsized risks to create his or her fortune, these types of risks may not be appropriate for maintaining and building the family fortune. Determining how much risk the family is willing and able to assume and how much volatility they can withstand is key to formulating a portfolio strategy that can deliver the required returns with an acceptable level of risk. Once an acceptable risk-return profile is developed, benchmarks can be established for tracking the portfolio's performance.

Next, it is extremely important to understand the historical norms of returns in various asset classes and what drives them. For example, for the 210 years of stock returns studied by legendary Wharton professor Jeremy Siegal, the real return on a broadly diversified portfolio of stocks has averaged 6.6% per year. There are two main drivers of asset class returns—inflation and growth. When growth is slower than expected, stocks go down. When inflation is higher than expected, bonds go down. When inflation is lower than expected, bonds go up. In the competitive world of money management, performance is measured not by absolute returns but the returns relative to some benchmark. For stocks and bonds, these benchmarks include the S&P 500 Index, the Wilshire 5000, the global bond index, and the latest "style" indexes popular on Wall Street. But there is a crucial difference about investing compared with virtually any other competitive activity: Most of us have no chance of being as adept as the group of individuals who practice for hours to hone their skills.

Step 3: determine asset allocation: Selecting from various asset classes and investment options, the investor can allocate assets in a way that achieves optimum diversification while targeting the expected returns. The investor can also assign percentages to various asset classes, including stocks, bonds, cash, and alternative investments, based on an acceptable range of volatility for the portfolio.

The asset allocation strategy is based on a snapshot of the family's current situation and goals and is usually adjusted over long periods of time. Single-family offices seeking to preserve and grow generational wealth often look for large macro trends starting with demographics and large economic shifts. For example, by 2060, India's economy is projected to be larger than China's because of its greater population growth. India is forecasted to produce about one-quarter of world GDP from 2040 through the rest of this century. Further, while Africa will remain a small part of the world economy until 2070, it is expected to then expand rapidly, reaching 14%, the same size as the economy of China, by the end of the century. How these types of transformations inform a family's asset allocation will be important questions that need to be asked and answered in determining optimal, long-term plans.

Step 4: select investment options: Individual investments are selected based on the parameters of the asset allocation strategy. The specific investment type selected depends in large part on the investor's preference for active or passive management. While active and passive are commonly used terms in the investment field, they can be a misnomer.

The range of investment options is wide and deep and requires true expertise to understand each. Understanding hedge funds, REITs (real estate investment trusts), private equity, public stocks, bonds, precious metals, commodities, and so forth is not a passive exercise. Constructing a proper portfolio of investments to achieve the family's goals require study, time, and patience. No one can consistently predict the rise and fall of any market for an asset class. As hedge fund manager Ray Dalio says, "He who lives by the crystal ball will eat shattered glass."

History is full of unpredictable and scary events, and these events impact the returns of various asset classes. The stock market is arguably the most studied of all of the asset markets and certainly garners the most popular press.

On average, corrections in the stock market occur about once a year since 1900. When a market falls by at least 10% from its peak, it is called a correction, a bland and neutral term, but even for an experienced investor, it can be unsettling. When any market falls by at least 20% from its peak, it is called a bear market. And bears are certainly scary.

Less than 20% of all corrections turn into bear markets and, historically, bear markets occur every three to five years. As discussed earlier, time is one of the big psychological hurdles to being successful in investment management. The greatest danger is being out of the market. Mohnish Pabrai tells us that investing is a waiting game. According to him, you do not make money when you buy an asset and you do not make money by selling it. You make money by investing in undervalued assets, then waiting for the price to converge with its true intrinsic value.

Step 5: monitor, measure, and rebalance: Investment management is not a one-and-done deal—it requires ongoing assessments and adjustments as the family goes through different stages. This includes monitoring the investments and measuring the portfolio's performance relative to the benchmarks.

It is necessary to report investment performance at regular intervals, typically quarterly, and to review the portfolio plan annually. Once a year, the family's situation and goals undergo a review to determine if there have been any significant changes. The portfolio review then determines if the allocation is still on target to track the family's risk-reward profile. If it is not, then the portfolio can be rebalanced, selling investments that have reached their targets, and buying investments that offer greater upside potential. After all the above points have been followed, the investor needs to keep monitoring the portfolio management performance at an appropriate interval going forward.

As noted, there are many other systematic processes that characterize high-performing single-family offices. Let us consider wealth planning.

Wealth Planning

When it comes to wealth planning, there is a comprehensive, yet flexible systematic planning process that incorporates the latest industry knowledge. It is known as the Virtuous

Cycle. Operationally, the Virtuous Cycle is composed of six steps (Exhibit 7.2). While we can identify distinct steps in the Virtuous Cycle, everything must be customized to each family member and what is important to them.

EXHIBIT 7.2: The Virtuous Cycle

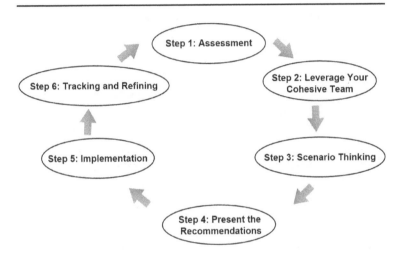

Step 1: Assessment: Wealth planning is all about each family member and what matters to them—their self-interests. The power of wealth planning is negated without having a deep understanding of the particular wishes and trepidations of particular family members and the people involved or affected by the planning decisions. Taking a close look at the fact-finders used by the great majority of professionals, we see they tend to be skewed by their narrow focus toward detailing assets and liabilities. Most of these tools fail to adequately address the self-interests of these family members.

We want to strongly emphasize the central and foundational role of the human element. First and foremost, it is because of the human element that you can build a high-performing single-family office. For example, your ability to determine the self-interests of family members enables you to uncover latent needs.

Failing to identify latent needs results in subpar wealth planning and, therefore, poor results. All too often, the complications from not addressing latent needs happen down the road, requiring costly revisions to wealth plans that are sometimes impossible to change. With a deep understanding of the family members, you tap the knowledge and capabilities of your cohesive team.

Step 2: Leverage your cohesive team: We have discussed the need and nature of a cohesive team. Just to restate: There are no polymaths when it comes to delivering the highest-quality advice to successful families. No one is a master at all the various types of specialized wealth planning. Your cohesive team works to help ensure you are always able to deliver superior results to the family.

Your ability to manage your cohesive team is central to building a high-performing single-family office and is readily apparent when it comes to wealth planning. It is your understanding of the capabilities and the self-interests of these specialists that produce superior results for the family. Left to their druthers, the various experts will tend to see the needs and wants of the family solely through the lens of their expertise. For instance, the lawyer thinks in terms of trusts, structures, and strategies, while the life insurance specialist finds the answers in life insurance. Since most of them probably never will, you need to concentrate on the self-interests of the family.

Step 3: Scenario thinking: With knowledge of family member self-interests in hand and the ability to leverage your cohesive team, the next step in the process is scenario thinking. Simply put, this is a method of generating alternative futures. This is when all the "What if?" questions are asked and answered.

To give you a feel for this, the following are some "What if?" questions we have addressed:

- "What if I die early while the children are young? Who will decide when they should have uninhibited access to the money?"

- "What if my family—they all do not get along too well—decide to fight over the money starting World War III after I'm gone?"

- "What if I want to pay the least possible taxes on my investments without having to give up how the money is managed?"

- "What if the kids from my first, second, and third marriages cause problems for my current wife and kids?"

- "What if the money I want to go to my side of the family is hijacked by the guardians of my children?"

- "What if I want to benefit certain charitable causes forever, and do not want future generations to make changes?"

- "What if the children decide they never have to do anything once they inherit?"

- "What if my trustee starts to do things that are not in the best interests of my family?"

- "What if I want to leave money to my boyfriend, but I don't want my wife or children to know?"

- "What if someone wants to take advantage of us when we're a lot older and not as with it?"

- "What if the charities I support take a different political turn, one I find repulsive?"

- "What if I want to sell divisions in my company—how do I avoid paying capital gains taxes?"

- "What if I want to reinvest in my company for my children, take out the money we need to live, and lower my personal tax rate?"

- "What if someone intentionally falls in my building, hurts himself, and sues?"

- "What if my idiot son is swept off his feet by a bottle-blond, buxom fortune-hunter?"

- "What if I start to become senile and don't know it?"

- "What if my husband decides to remarry when I am gone, and that person is only looking at dollar signs?"

- "What if my kids are unprepared to manage the money when they get it?"

- "What if I want to expand my business to other countries and want to make sure I legally do not have to pay all the taxes?"

And the list goes on and on and on. Wealth planning can address all these "What if?" questions. There are a number of different ways to deal with each of these matters, but the best approaches are always predicated on the particulars of the situation and the self-interests of the family.

From the meaningful possible outcomes devised in this step, the most viable course or courses of action are selected to discuss with the family. This set of possibilities might not be the final answer because it is critical to constantly confirm what the family wants to achieve and match it up to what will be considered. Still, with recommendations ready, it is time to discuss them.

Step 4: Present the recommendations: At this point in the process, you and members of your cohesive team discuss the various scenarios and recommendations with the family. It is essential that they understand—in broad strokes to excruciating detail, depending on their preferences—how the recommended solutions may enable them to achieve their self-interests, as well as the conditions they impose.

Many professionals do not communicate effectively; some of the smartest professionals are unable to discuss their recommendations without relying on mind-numbing jargon or talking over the heads of their clients. Your facility with the Everyone Wins Process empowers you to most effectively communicate the concepts and value of your recommendations.

Step 5: Implementation: Once the family has selected how they want to proceed, you and your cohesive team make things happen. Implementation—taking action—is typically straightforward.

The reason implementation is so straightforward is that by this point all the hurdles have been identified and the approaches to surmounting them have been specified. This does not mean implementation is easy; it is often a great deal of work. However, it is familiar ground and is something the high-performing single-family office and the chosen external experts should be able to do extremely well. The key skillsets in implementation are persistence and precision, not the more draining intuition and analysis.

Step 6: Tracking and refining: As with every process you use, tracking is essential. It is wise to ensure that the family's wealth planning stays current and that it achieves the results the family wants. Therefore, you need to continually monitor the situation and work with family members and your cohesive team to make modifications as required. When new legal strategies or financial products, for example, are developed and validated, you might need to bring selected solutions that are potentially beneficial to the family's attention.

At high-performing single-family offices, wealth planning is a continuous process of refining. If the family's wealth plan becomes dated, they and those who are important to them lose out.

Stress Testing

Stress testing is an in-depth evaluation of the actions the single-family office or the family independently has taken or is considering. It can lead to a reaffirmation or a change of course.

High-performing single-family offices regularly stress test. It is an astute way to help ensure that all involved are making smart decisions and to confirm the family is working with truly capable internal and external experts. Also, stress testing is an effective way to find previously unseen problems and make necessary changes to get the results the family is looking for before it is too late.

Stress testing is valuable because many less-than-adept professionals seek to be hired or do business with your single-family offices. Although these professionals want to do a good job, they may not be up to the job. They are likely to make mistakes—some of these mistakes may be serious. Additionally, these subpar professionals are even more likely to miss meaningful opportunities the family may benefit from.

By definition, stress testing is a systematic way to evaluate whether the actions and decisions being made at the single-family office will deliver the results the family expects, help them achieve their interests, and ensure the family is not missing any meaningful opportunities (Exhibit 7.3):

- Avoiding potential economic and legal destructive situations
- Making sure you are benefitting from all possible opportunities

EXHIBIT 7.3: Stress Testing

Consider the following situation: A parent's will stated that the youngest son, currently six years of age, would, on turning 12, receive an inheritance of slightly more than US $250 million.

Who would hand this much money over to a 12-year-old? Not many families would hand over a quarter of a billion dollars to a 12-year-old and, as it turned out, this family would not think of doing so either.

The technical failure was the transposition of two numbers. The will should have stated that the son will inherit the fortune at 21 years of age, not 12. Again, who would hand this much money over to a 21-year-old? How many families would entrust US $250 million to a 21-year-old when that person is only six years old today? We pointed out that, in fact, it might actually be safer to give a 12-year-old US $250 million than give a 21-year-old that amount.

Some very successful families might hand a quarter of a billion dollars to a 21-year-old without restriction, but this family was appalled by the idea. Evidently, there was a serious breakdown in communication between the family and the advisors involved in the estate plan.

Because of stress testing, the family's estate plan was dramatically adjusted and updated. At the moment, it is tightly aligned with the family's overall agenda and the son will inherit substantial wealth in a very disciplined manner—but not a quarter of a billion dollars (US) when he turns 12 or 21. The estate plan delivers the framework and structure for creating a dynasty while insulating family members from losing wealth through taxes, litigation, or divorce.

Stress testing is also becoming very prevalent in ensuring that certain lifestyle services are as good as they can be and on target. One family, for example, engaged us because they were concerned about the physical safety of their children.

The children all traveled extensively by private jet with close protection personnel. In order to stress test the protective cocoon of the children, a team of professionals was assembled and charged—conceptually—with kidnapping the children. The kidnapping was meticulously planned and extensively documented, but never actually carried out. The aim was to identify weaknesses in the actions being taken to protect the children. In this case, a handful of high-probability kidnap opportunities were identified.

Some families stress test the security of their homes. In one situation, we arranged for a team of ex-cons and former police officers to see if they could burgle selected residences when the owners and staff were not present. The owners had legally absolved the to-be burglars of any liability and arrangements were made with the authorities. Tellingly, the burglar team had little problem entering the various houses and—in principle, but not actually—walking away with the contents of safes as well as precious artwork. Subsequently, the owners significantly upgraded the security of these residences.

It is clear that stress testing is becoming much more normative and is not restricted to wealth management. Because successful families want results, stress testing will be applied to an expanding set of actions.

The stress testing process: There is a systematic way to go about stress testing (Exhibit 7.4):

EXHIBIT 7.4: The Stress Testing Process

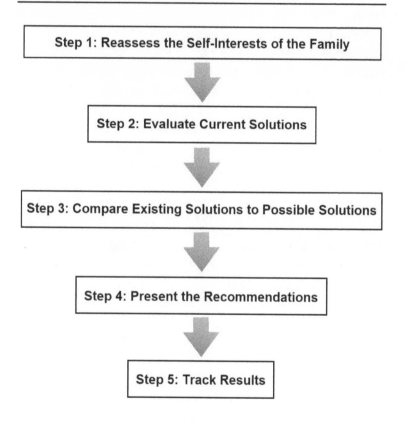

- **Step 1: Reassess the self-interests of the family:** This involves being attentive to the human element. By using the Everyone Wins Process, you are constantly refining your understanding of what matters to the family as well as what does not. Many times, it is the human element as opposed to technical matters that prompts changes in investment selection and wealth planning as well as changes in lifestyle services. It is common for a family's circumstances to change; what once was on point no longer necessitates modifying their investment portfolios or their wealth planning and so forth.

- **Step 2: Evaluate current solutions**: With a full understanding of the family's self-interests, high-performing single-family offices—relying on their cohesive teams—will evaluate the solutions currently being employed. Four common components of the process include:

  - Determining the degree of current alignment with the self-interests of the family

  - Working the assumptions by changing the "what ifs" of the scenarios

  - Assessing possible synergies

  - Calculating the cost-structures

- **Step 3: Compare existing solutions to possible solutions:** Based on the evaluations of existing solutions, you will make reasoned comparisons with other possibilities. Such options need to be able to deliver either more aligned results or a better way of achieving the self-interests of the family. As always, the aim is to produce superior results.

- **Step 4: Present the recommendations:** Here, you guide the family on how to proceed. If you find the solutions being used are on target and of high quality, the recommendation is to stay the course. If the stress testing uncovers what is generally called a *system failure*, then the answer is to quickly take a different course of action. Sometimes, the experts being engaged need to be replaced. Many times, stress testing will identify areas where slight modifications can make the current solutions more effective.

- **Step 5: Track results**: Remember to constantly track results. You want to make certain any changes you make are indeed delivering superior results. You also want to make sure the family's self-interests and expectations are in sync with what is presently happening.

When you are not 100% comfortable with a course of action, consider stress testing. If you feel there might (just might) be something you should be doing but are not, then consider stress testing. By stress testing, you will either confirm that you are on target or identify corrections that will put you on target. This is why stress testing is a service provided by all types of high-performing family offices.

Conclusion

Along with the human element and a cohesive team, being systematic distinguishes high-performing family offices from their not-as-effective peers. Systematic processes, like the ones we discussed here—investment management, wealth planning, and stress testing—help produce superior results. In a nutshell, the intent is to consistently be thoughtful and methodical.

When senior management implements systematic processes, they are much less likely to let gut feelings, unsubstantiated ideas, or family dynamics act as anchors holding them down. This does not mean that they are bound to the specifics of the systematic processes. The steps we discussed in investment management, wealth planning, and stress testing are not set in stone. Flexibility is important, as it allows you to adapt to changing circumstances. Still, you need to be rigorous if you want to build a high-performing single-family office.

What can be the biggest obstacle or the biggest driver in building a high-performing single-family office? The answer is the successful family. As we said, a single-family office is all about the family. Remember the mantra: *family first*. In the next section, we look at some of your self-interests and a few scenarios where the attitude and preferences of family members are consequential.

PART III

The Family in the Single-Family Office

CHAPTER 8

Getting Hired and Compensated

COMPENSATING INNER-CIRCLE SINGLE-FAMILY office senior executives is one of the most important issues facing successful families and likely one of the most important considerations in someone—like you—taking the job. Compensation is often the primary motivator. Unless, of course, you are family, then things can get complicated (see below).

In many ways, the ability of the single-family office to fulfill the family office promise ties back to the quality of senior management. We have found that the compensation arrangements—often more than anything else—is what determines the quality of non-family senior management at any single-family office.

For a relatively few talented and motivated professionals, working in a single-family office can be quite lucrative. Becoming seriously wealthy by working in a single-family office is not the norm, but it is a slowly growing trend. The payouts coupled with their often-distinctive working environments increasingly make inner-circle senior executive positions in single-family offices quite attractive for exceptional professionals.

Before addressing compensation, it is useful to understand how most non-family senior executives currently find positions with single-family offices.

How Non-Family Professionals Connect with Single-Family Offices

Talented professionals connect with single-family offices in a number of ways. It is important to recognize that multiple approaches are used by single-family offices to fill senior management positions. The most prevalent ways are . . .

- **Referrals from professionals currently engaged by the single-family office:** This is a well-used, proven-effective approach the family uses to source inner-circle single-family office senior executives. Successful families recognize that, within the private wealth universe, leading experts know many highly talented professionals in a variety of fields. These connections are leveraged when a family is looking to hire senior executives for their single-family offices. Getting introductions from these professionals proves to be an exceptional risk mitigation strategy. Relying on professionals with whom they are presently working is the most common approach to finding talent.

- **Recruiters:** More and more recruiters are becoming increasingly important for successful families looking for talent as single-family offices become more professionalized. As such, families are turning to recruiters to find and screen capable professionals for senior management positions. When working with a recruiter, it is useful for you to carefully jointly map out the way you are positioned. This can lead to a better fit as well as a more lucrative compensation arrangement.

- **Previous experience with the professional:** This is where the professional worked for the single-family office as an external expert. This approach is also a way for the family to be confident in the talent it is considering hiring as a senior executive. Having worked with the family in some capacity provides them an understanding of your capabilities and verifies that there is chemistry with family members.

Additional ways of connecting include referrals from senior management at other single-family offices, networking activities and events, referrals from other people, and unsolicited approaches. However, all in all, these additional ways of connecting tend to be inconsequential. The big three ways of connecting are when you are recommended by some other professional they are working with, through the efforts of recruiters, or because you know them due to having done business with them before.

Become a thought leader: If you want to work for a successful family as an inner-circle senior executive in their single-family office, you would be wise to be recognized by other professionals for your expertise. Furthermore, being known to work with the wealthy and having insights into the family office universe increases your chances—sometimes dramatically.

This positioning would also better position you with recruiters. You would more often be seen as a possible candidate and you are making it easier for the recruiters to communicate your value to interested families.

What we are talking about is being a *thought leader*. As such, you are recognized by selected audiences, such as the wealthy, your peers, and certain other professionals, as the go-to authority for your expertise. Essential to being a thought leader is being an expert and a willingness to freely share. The following 4-step process can help you become a thought leader (Exhibit 8.1):

- **Step 1: Commit to becoming a thought leader**: Above all, becoming a thought leader requires commitment. This includes commitments of time, money, and effort. It cannot be something you pay attention to now and again.

- **Step 2a: Identify your expertise**: This is all about what you want to be recognized for. Since you are probably quite adept in several related areas, you are going to have to narrow your field of expertise down. It is better to be an expert on cross-border planning than on wealth planning, writ large. Being seen as an authority on mediating family disputes can be more effective than being known for working with successful families.

- **Step 2b: Identify your audiences**: Not only do you need to be targeted when it comes to your expertise, you also want to focus in on particular audiences. For example, "rich people" is an incredibly broad description and can thus prove disappointing. In contrast, focusing on "wealthy business-owning families with operations in more than one jurisdiction" will let you much more readily be seen as the go-to professional for this audience. Certainly, if you want to work in or with single-family offices, this cohort becomes your prime audience.

- **Step 3: Produce and share your thought leadership content**: You have to package up your expertise in ways that other people can benefit from. If you are not good at creating content, you can often generate the same impact by carefully curating content. Then, you need to share your thought leadership content with your chosen audiences. This can take a wide variety of forms, such as blogs and presentations. Often, the nature of the content lends itself to how to best share it.

- **Step 4: Track results**: In putting the resources into becoming a thought leader, you want to make it work for you. The easiest way to evaluate this is to see if your material is being shared beyond your efforts and if people are contacting you in reference to your thought leadership content.

EXHIBIT 8.1: Become a Thought Leader

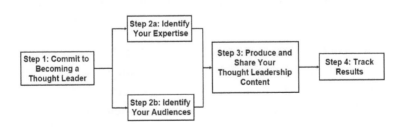

Being a thought leader is beneficial for professionals aside from helping them get positions at single-family offices or enhancing their responsibilities for the successful family. The wealthy want to work with the very best. By being a thought leader, the audiences you concentrate on will see you as the expert they want to work with. Being a thought leader is an extremely powerful way for professionals and other providers to generate new business.

When You Are Family

Any problem connecting with the single-family office evaporates when you are family. Instead, the matters of qualifications and nepotism can become telling points of contention. Some of the questions that arise are . . .

- Are you getting the position because you are capable or because you are "blood?"
- How will other senior executives see you?
- Is there any contention within the family of you being responsible for them and the family's wealth?
- Are you being held to the same standards as other senior executives?
- Are your qualifications as good for the position as a non-family member?

When the single-family office is not an autocracy with you being the autocrat, family politics can make your life complicated. It then falls to you to understand your family's self-interests and those of senior management and respond accordingly.

Family history often plays into decision-making. Generally speaking, it can be more arduous and tangled for you to build a high-performing single-family office than a non-family member. For instance, one family member senior executive got a lot of pushback from other family members because he used to wet his bed when he was six years old. That was more than 30 years ago and is not a problem today. It is just that some of his siblings and cousins seem to associate this behavior with his ability to manage money.

Being a family member joining your single-family office can be a two-edged sword. In one single-family office, the retiring executive director was replaced by a second-generation family member. Being the son of the patriarch certainly was the primary reason he got the job. He knew that some of his family lobbied against him getting the post, claiming he was unseasoned and would show favoritism. He, therefore, had to prove that he was indeed capable and fair. All in all, he felt tremendous pressure to deliver.

How you connect with single-family offices and successful families is one thing. How you are compensated is another.

Compensating Senior Management

When we were conducting extensive compensation surveys and providing compensation consulting, we received different types of inquiries . . .

- **From family members:** "How do we pay talented non-family senior executives fairly, but toward the lower end of the range?"

- **From prospective non-family senior executives:** "How can I get paid for my contributions to the single-family office and the family, but toward the higher end of the range?"

- **From family members in senior management positions**: "What type and level of compensation is justifiable?"

- **From family members who are not directly involved in their single-family offices**: "Why do we have to pay family members if they are part of senior management? They're family!"

Different compensation studies in the field of single-family offices are coming up with similar findings showing a certain level of consistency when it comes to paying senior management. This is a function of the increasing levels of professionalism and a greater reliance on recruiters and human resource consultants. While compensation research can offer guidance, the many situations we worked on all had their unique issues requiring bespoke compensation arrangements.

When it comes to compensating senior management, in our experience, we found ourselves mediating an agreement. We often worked on developing complex compensation agreements where people were paid based on their performance.

There are other scenarios where compensation is much more straightforward, such as when an accounting professional is brought on board to only handle administrative services. When it comes to senior management, there are three main approaches.

Compensation arrangements: There are basically three different arrangements to compensate inner-circle single-family office senior executives:

- **The employee model:** Inner-circle senior executives receive a salary and a discretionary bonus. Compensation of a few hundred thousand dollars US is most common, though numbers can vary greatly depending on jurisdiction.

- **The participatory model:** Senior executives are rewarded strictly on performance—their contributions to the single-family office and the successful family. Compensation can range from zero—nothing at all—to tens of millions of US dollars. In our experience, there have been rare situations where senior executives earned more than US $30 million in one year.

- **The hybrid model:** This is a combination of the other two compensation arrangements. There is usually a base of around US $100,000—sometimes a little more or a little less. However, the participation in investments or the calculable results achieved by the single-family office is where the senior executives can earn millions.

Let us take a closer look at these models . . .

The employee model: The compensation for inner-circle single-family office senior executives under the employee model is quite stable year in and year out. For a solid percentage of senior executives, this is very attractive.

While the base salary might go up slightly, the bonus is discretionary and often a function of what is happening at the single-family office. Because it is usually determined by how some family members think things are going plus the "what have you done for me lately" attitude, the bonus can vary considerably.

The big drawback to the employee model is that it can be seen as limiting senior management's earning ability. It often proves to be a very touchy issue for those senior executives directly involved in investing for the family. In good times, they tend to feel shortchanged. In bad times, they never seem to bring up the topic of compensation.

The participatory model: While the employee model is fairly straightforward, the participatory and hybrid models can be complex. The greater your compensation is a function of a participation arrangement, the greater the possibility you can become personally wealthy.

Commonly, the monies inner-circle senior executives receive tend to vary considerably, but the upside is potentially considerable. It is *the* way you can become seriously wealthy in your own right working for a single-family office, but it comes with the greatest financial risks. The participatory model is based on pre-set (usually immutable) performance criteria.

Participatory models tend to most easily tie to investment performance. It is easier to see quantifiable results when it comes to investment performance compared to wealth planning and family support services. When compensation is linked to investment performance, there are usually components of the arrangement, such as clawbacks and vesting schedules, that help ensure long-term commitments. Otherwise, you can decide to stack all your chips on a long-shot bet. If that investment comes through you will be rich and quit the single-family office. If that investment fails, you are fired and the family loses heavily.

Over the years, we have come up with various ways to make

the participatory model work for other family concerns such as wealth planning and the ongoing management responsibilities of the high-performing single-family office. All of these scenarios centered on exceeding the expectations of the family when it came to specific areas of expertise. It is worthwhile to note that senior executives whose participatory compensation is based on non-investment services are less likely to earn as much compared to what can be earned when the participatory model is tied to money management.

The hybrid model: To mitigate some of the financial risks of the participatory model and to provide greater upside than the employee model, there is the hybrid model. By providing a comparatively lower base compensation, senior executives are not as likely to end up in "do or die" type situations. Also, there is the possibility for substantial upside, but less than if it was a pure participatory model.

When You Are Family

Compensation arrangements tend to be much trickier when you are family. If you are completely in charge, you can make your compensation anything you want. However, founders of single-family offices that are running them tend not to take compensation. On the other hand, when you are an inner-circle senior executive and there are other senior executives as well as multiple family members providing oversight, compensation may be very important.

The best scenario is when your compensation is commensurate with the position. That is, you are being paid—with whatever model—as a non-family member would be paid. Not more (rarely the case) and not less (much more common).

In one situation, the family did not want to—in any way—compensate the family member responsible for managing the family's considerable aggregate wealth. Their reasoning was that she is investing her own wealth and would therefore do a good job. Having the family fortune to manage enabled her to benefit from the amount of assets the single-family office controlled—very true. As the individual responsible for investing the family's monies, she was doing a great job.

However, she feels cheated, as she works incessantly to generate great investment returns while her two siblings are perpetually vacationing and they receive the same financial benefits from the single-family office as she does. At the same time, she does want to run the money because the investment performance of the single-family office when it was relying on non-family members was pretty bad. The notion of pulling her share of the family fortune out and managing it on her own, while appealing, is impossible because of legal restrictions.

Bottom line: The best approach is for your compensation as an inner-circle senior executive to be in lockstep with that of a non-family member doing the same job.

Conclusion

With the explosive growth in the number of single-family offices worldwide, there is complementary demand for talented professionals to manage them or provide expertise. If you are not family, you need to connect with single-family offices. The most common way to do this is through the professionals you know who are working with successful families and single-family offices. But you have to stand out, which is why being a thought leader can be helpful.

Well-developed and implemented compensation plans are

the optimal way to attract, retain, and motivate exceptional professionals who are foundational to the success of a single-family office.

While the employee model is most common, participatory and hybrid models are potentially the most lucrative for senior executives.

Being a family member makes connecting with the single-family office easy, but your compensation arrangement can be complicated.

The mantra of the single-family office is *Family First*, which can prove troublesome when you have to deal with dysfunctional family members. We take a look at these complications in the next chapter.

CHAPTER 9

Dealing with Family Dysfunction

Y OU MIGHT BE one of the very rare exceptions. Your family—immediate family or extended family—is populated by completely well-adjusted, emotionally stable, problem-free members. There might never be any drama in your family life.

Our families are not. We admit to them being dysfunctional. Moreover, the world is filled with dysfunctional families.

While dysfunctional families dominate the family landscape, you have to put this fact in perspective. There is an extensive hierarchy of dysfunction from personality quirks that do not meaningfully impact the person or family to examples of destructive, malignant narcissism, and from disagreements to all-out take-no-prisoners family warfare.

Family dysfunction does not have to get in the way of you building a high-performing single-family office. Then again, it could make the endeavor impossible. Too often, family members, professionals, and those researching single-family offices pretend that family dynamics are not as critical as they are to the success of the single-family office.

The Impact of Great Wealth

Seventeen times in rehab. Six different consulting psychiatrists. Twelve arrests; no convictions. More than thirty lawsuits that never went to trial. All speed bumps for this 28-year-old. Nothing is going to slow him down for long. That is, until he accidentally kills someone or, more likely, unintentionally kills himself.

With every crisis, the family marshaled resources and protected him. Money buys the best legal talent, top-notch public relations specialists, and—desperately needed—crisis managers (and fixers of varying stripes).

Consider another situation where one family member plotted to kill his entire family. He was having dreams that his family was plotting his demise. Now, the ONLY evidence he had of their plotting was his dreams. The literally dozens of investigators he hired to find proof were unable to come up with any evidence. The police also discounted his claims. In his view, all this only proved—absolutely proved—his family was plotting to kill him. They were just being very sneaky about it.

He built himself a bunker so he would be safe and tried to hire assassins over the Internet to eliminate those family members he was certain wanted his elimination. (Note: trying to hire assassins over the Internet will only bring you to the attention of the authorities.) He has a team of lawyers who are doing an excellent job of keeping him out of jail as he spends family money to destroy the family business and thereby destroy the family.

It is not that family dysfunction is produced by great wealth, but great wealth can accentuate family dysfunction by enabling psychological problems to perpetuate and potentially intensify. Significant wealth can be used to cover up a lot of sins. It can act as a shield keeping people from getting the help they need.

Not all dysfunction is as extreme as these two examples—though some is a lot worse. What you need to realize is that you are or will be dealing with the family, which means you are or will be dealing with some level of dysfunction. How much this affects you and your work depends on many factors. As part of the inner circle, you will not be able to avoid having to deal with some of the family's issues.

Dysfunctional Relatives

Sometimes siblings and children from successful families can be described as *dysfunctional*. While unfortunate, dysfunctional family members who only do damage to themselves are not as problematic as those who lash out at the family. While the former likely emotionally hurt loved ones, the latter evidence cruelty and damage.

Problems for the family arise when these dysfunctional family members misbehave. The most serious problems for the family come about when these family members are engaging in various forms of immoral and illegal activities ranging from drug use to acts of violence and in some way pull the family into the ordeal. It is these family members that we will address.

Nowadays, some dysfunctional family members appear on social media sites. They are seeking adulation for their bad behavior. It is not that they do not care what other people think. Instead, they get a thrill out of shocking others and basking in the attention—even if it is negative. The least problematic but most common issue that arises from this type of behavior is reputational risk to the family.

Inflicting pain and damage: In contrast, most dysfunctional family members are living lives out of the limelight where they strive to be ruthlessly Machiavellian or indulge in excesses that hurt themselves, their families, and other people. They are regularly in conflict with society, requiring their families to come to their rescue in one form or another. What is telling is that—for the most part—their families do indeed arrive with the intent of "rescuing" them from the deleterious situations they created.

Even when their actions are directed against the interests and well-being of the family, they often avoid any harsh consequences. These outcomes foster a sense of invulnerability in dysfunctional family members and considerable animosity from other family members, creating a cycle of family harm.

Dysfunctional Family Members and the Single-Family Office

For many successful families, their single-family office is a family business. It is the means for them to take care of themselves and future generations. When dysfunctional family members are involved in overseeing or running the single-family office, problems large and small (mostly large) ensue.

Dysfunctional family members are actually pretty easy to spot. They exploit their single-family office and their family's wealth, connections, and business interests for personal gain to the detriment of other family members and other people—including you. Their activities put pressure on other family members and hurt the effectiveness of their single-family office as well as all other family business interests.

Where the family members overseeing or managing the single-family office are determined and more autocratic than not, dysfunctional family members tend not to have control or influence over the family's wealth. However, many families want their family members to get along and work together, which can mean the dysfunctional ones end up running unchecked. In these scenarios, relationships usually suffer and financial decisions can be skewed negatively as the family tries to hash out the conflicts.

Even though everyone would like the family to work together in a supportive and constructive way, that just does not happen in situations where there are dysfunctional family members. Remember, they are usually self-absorbed and commonly feel authorized to do what they like, no matter who might get hurt along the way.

The need to take action: What makes these situations especially complicated is that most families have a hard time reining in disruptive and oppressive family members. Many parents, for example, generally have a difficult time effectively punishing the negative behavior of their children. When those children are involved in their single-family offices, the problems are magnified. We have heard statements like these:

- "He's just going through a phase."
- "She didn't mean it when she said it."
- "All he needs is a little more growing up."

The reality is that it is not a phase if it has been going on for more than a decade. She very much does mean it and it is causing the family to splinter. And at 49 years old, if one still needs to "grow up," there is a good chance it is not going to happen.

While working with one successful family, we advised that they prune a major branch from the family tree—something they would not even consider. Another family was putting their faith in the fourth generation because they thought the third generation was a lost cause. These families recognized the dysfunction but were unwilling to take required actions. This scenario plays out the same way in many successful families. However, some actions can be taken that are for the good of the family and the dysfunctional family member.

Wealth planning with dysfunctional family members: A powerful way to address some dysfunctional family members is with wealth planning. For example, in certain cases, leaving money to problem-ridden heirs can be an actual death sentence. There was a successful family where one of the children had a severe opioid addiction. When his father died, the estate was divided evenly among the children, with each of them getting their inheritance unencumbered. The other two inheritors bought the addicted one out of the family businesses. Within a year, the addicted inheritor died of an overdose.

A variety of wealth planning strategies can be used to insulate the family and mitigate the impact of self-ruinous and destructive behaviors. Using trusts resulting in the oversight of a child's inheritance is a common and relatively easy way to protect him or her and other people. Of course, the best way to use trusts will depend on each particular situation, and trusts in these scenarios usually have asset protection advantages, which also must be taken into account.

In certain situations, the nature of wealth planning to help deal with dysfunctional family members becomes more specialized. Where there are family businesses (including the single-family office) involved, matters of succession concerns and who gets what can lead to intense arguments. While there are different ways of addressing these matters, families often need to think through the various approaches and become comfortable with the most probable outcomes.

What is clear is that there are likely always going to be family members who behave in deleterious ways. The responsibility of dealing with them and, many times, rescuing them is more and more becoming the responsibility of the family's single-family office.

Dealing with Dysfunctional Family Members in Trouble

It happens with some frequency:

- Getting addicted to drugs, but it is okay because he says he can handle it

- Racing the high-powered sports car with police in close pursuit

- Sexually harassing the staff of the single-family office

- Starting (and losing) a bar fight that was captured by multiple cellphone cameras

- Hitting a police officer when drunk

- Hitting a police officer when not drunk

- Starting a small fire in a hotel room that became a big fire

- Accidentally pushing a person out of a window twice

- Stealing money and jewels from the family and giving them to the only girl who truly understands him

- Regularly physically abusing other family members

As a senior executive at the single-family office and part of the inner circle, it is very likely you might get pulled into situations where you have to help the family deal with dysfunctional family members. Dealing with the problems caused by them is often broadly conceptualized as a 4-step process (Exhibit 9.1):

- **Step 1: Crisis management**: Immediate problems need to be addressed. For example, if the family member was arrested, lawyers are required to arrange for bail or some other speedy solution. A public relations expert might be required. If there is a way to readily address damages, that approach must be identified and evaluated. In whatever ways possible, the situation has to be—as much as possible—diffused.

- **Step 2a: Situation problem management**: This is an extension of the previous step. The situation has been somewhat diffused, and action is now being taken to mitigate and fix the problems created by the family member. An expanded team of specialists may be required. At the end of this step, there is some form of resolution to the problems caused by the family member.

- **Step 2b: Problem management**: The family takes action to help their family member get help if needed. Some corrective action must also be taken to help ensure the situation—or some versions of the situation—does not repeat itself. For example, in the case of drug addiction, the family member almost always goes to a rehabilitation center. Sometimes, the families are able to adjust the financials to make it difficult or impossible for these family members to access their wealth when being destructive and harmful to themselves or other people.

- **Step 3: From dysfunctional family member to a responsible individual:** Many times, a longer-term strategy is conceived and implemented to help a family member become a stable, well-functioning capable individual. This is not to say that he or she will not make mistakes—everyone does. The aim—if nothing else—is to help the family member avoid repeating the actions that caused him or her and their family's significant problems. Part of the solution, if possible, is to control their access to family money until he or she is able to maturely and smartly make financial decisions.

- **Step 4: Track outcomes:** With all actions of the family, tracking is essential. The aim is to see if a course of action is working and if so, how well it is working. If progress is not being made, then additional remedial actions will be needed. Tracking results can prove very important in helping break through the wall of denial that can be seen in many dysfunctional family members.

EXHIBIT 9.1: Dealing with Dysfunctional Heirs in Trouble

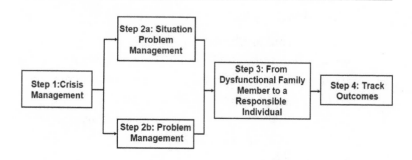

Dealing with a problem caused by dysfunctional family members and pursuing ways to help them is a complex process. Various experts are needed throughout the process, and determination from the family is a requirement. When incidents occur, the single-family offices are—more so than ever—getting involved in addressing them. Therefore, you may very well need to know how to help the family in these difficult times.

When You Are Family

Life can get complicated and problematic when you are family and have to deal with dysfunctional family members who remember you getting drunk in college or making a fool of yourself over an infatuation, or who use shared experiences to try to manipulate you. It is often the case that narcissistic and clever dysfunctional family members know how to pull all the right levers and push all the right buttons to get you to clean up the messes they make.

These dysfunctional family members, however, may never

take corrective action. For example, most parents will come to the aid of their children no matter what they have done. Having extensive resources means they can often be more protective and more enabling. If this is the case, it is very, very unlikely to change. Therefore, making sure a high-performing single-family office delivers superior results may entail accurately answering one question.

One question: Family history and dynamics come into play in any family business when family members are part of senior management and the single-family office is a family business. While it is never easy to accurately answer, the question you can ask yourself when making decisions concerning family is . . .

If this person was not related to me,
what would I do in this situation?

In answering this question, you are trying to be as objective as possible about the situation. Your aim is to make decisions that you believe are best for the family. You are aiming to take "family" out of your calculations. Your goal is to come up with a course of action that serves everyone to the greatest extent possible.

What we often find happens when family members who are inner-circle senior executives in their single-family office answer this question is that they recognize the extent to which they are enabling their dysfunctional family members. Sometimes it takes a while before they see this, but over time they become more aware of how they may be perpetuating the problem. While this realization may not cause anything to change—the family will still bail out the dysfunctional family member—the awareness lets people be honest with themselves.

Conclusion

It is quite common in successful families—and all families for that matter—for some of the family members to have serious problems that adversely impact their lives and often cause serious problems for the family. Many of these dysfunctional family members can prove disastrous as they can derail businesses and investments. They can diminish the value of their family's single-family office. Moreover, they can cause considerable emotional angst to other family members.

For the sake of the family and—very importantly—for the sake of dysfunctional family members, there are steps families can take to better manage these situations. Part of the solution is being adept at wealth planning to ensure the dysfunctional family members do not squander funds or use their wealth to hurt themselves or others. Often, a proactive approach to crisis management enables families to help dysfunctional family members in times of crises and thereafter. It can also help buttress the adverse complications of their counter-productive behavior on the family.

Many successful families think in terms of generations. We turn to this topic next.

CHAPTER 10

Establishing a Family Dynasty

A GROWING NUMBER OF successful families seek to perpetuate their fortunes and their business interests, as well as their stature and family cohesiveness across generations. What many of them are aiming to establish is a *family dynasty*.

There are many ways to think about dynastic wealth. The definition we use when researching the concept is . . .

A family dynasty is a cohesive economic entity where the perpetuation of family wealth, values, and objectives lasts for five or more generations.

What is important to keep in mind is that a family dynasty is not only when the family across generations share financial interests, they also have the same values and goals. It is because of these shared values and objectives that there is a commitment to the family.

Family dynasties are multi-generational families that have shared businesses and investment portfolios that support the family members. Because we are going out generations, there are likely to be multiple branches that complicate sustaining the dynasty.

When it comes to facilitating dynastic wealth, the idea is for the family fortune, the advantages of wealth, and a shared worldview to reach at least the great-great-grandchildren of the founders. The intent is that, although the founders are no longer alive, their legacy in the form of financial capital, human capital, and social capital continues on.

The Role of the High-Performing Single-Family Office

Among many successful families, single-family offices are seen as instrumental in creating and perpetuating family dynasties. One of the core benefits of a high-performing single-family office is that it leverages the power of the family's aggregate wealth.

To reiterate, the ability to use the family's combined wealth gives it a distinct and powerful advantage in a number of ways including:

- Accessing and negotiating with professionals and other providers to get exceptional cost-effective solutions
- Leveraging the aggregate financial capital of the family to build a larger fortune
- Receiving preferential treatment in various life scenarios; in effect, receiving world-class services and moving to the head of the line
- The ability to invest longer-term—across generations

For those successful families who are thinking in terms of a family dynasty, high-performing single-family offices deliver additional advantages such as:

- Fostering family cohesion
- Providing educational resources for inheritors to prepare them to take over
- Addressing dysfunctional family members in the context of the self-interests of the family

Critically, the single-family office can be a key part in making sure the values of the family persist. A percentage of successful families thinking in terms of family dynasties build their values and objectives into their single-family offices and lock them in using legal strategies and structures.

If the family is thinking in terms of a dynasty, you will see evidence of it in their actions. Furthermore, you will likely have to help family members think through issues and develop action plans that will affect future generations.

Let us consider some of the issues you will need to address.

Across the Generations

While some family fortunes are so immense they can last for many generations no matter what happens, these are usually the exceptions, not the rule. To build a family dynasty, you will need . . .

- Shared values and objectives
- An array of legal structures and agreements
- Ways to ensure accountability
- Significant financial resources

Over time, there are going to be continual changes in the business, social, political, and even physical environments. The successful family will need to adopt and, where possible, benefit from these changes.

At the same time, as the family goes into the second and later generations, the levels of complexity within the family tend to increase as a function of more family members. For instance, over generations, there are likely to be different family branches that result in greater diverse self-interests and demands. It, therefore, becomes more and more challenging to ensure family members work cooperatively, and that family values and objectives persist.

Without question, perpetuating a family dynasty requires keeping family self-interests aligned with the shared self-interests, including shared vision, goals, and values. It will also involve making sure there are sufficient funds to continue.

The need for family cohesiveness: Family dynasties are born from the entrepreneurial achievements of their founders. However, without further growing the wealth, most prospective family dynasties will falter because the monies will be divided and depleted as the number of heirs multiply. Of course, poor investments and uncontrolled spending will also destroy family wealth. Simply put, for most successful families to create family dynasties, they must continue to grow their commingled assets (see below).

With each passing generation, there are more branches of the family with their own agendas. Conflicts will arise as those not in control are at odds with family members responsible for making critical decisions, especially when it comes to managing the combined family wealth.

A possible complication is the preference for some family

members to take their share and go their own way. This is all the more likely, as there are more and more inheritors resulting in more personality clashes and more strong disagreements over investments.

When families fragment, they are more inclined to lose their wealth for diverse reasons. This is not to say that the family members will not be affluent, but the levels of wealth for individual family members may very well decline—sometimes significantly.

To perpetuate a family dynasty, family members need to anticipate the increase in heirs and dispersion of a percentage of the wealth.

Locking in family members: Sometimes founders and later generations have used legal structures and entities including trusts, foundations, corporations, and partnerships to cement a family dynasty. However, there are possible complications with locking in family members.

Forcing clever people to work together when they prefer not to can produce unintended consequences such as paranoia accompanied by sabotage. It is not unheard of for family members in these situations to be duplicitous and manipulative with the family.

Some of these legal structures and entities can pose problems for future generations. For example, a trust established by a founder might be totally out of sync with what is going on a generation or two later. The consequences are usually legal battles that only consume family monies while enriching lawyers.

The need to grow the family fortune: Over time—across generations—some family fortunes will end up under pressure.

As noted, one of the most significant pressures is when there is a growing cohort of inheritors all wanting what they see as their due. The conundrum is to keep the family fortune united and increase it to match the demands of the heirs.

We find that families striving to build and maintain dynasties want to provide both a financial foundation and a powerful legacy to future generations that matches or exceeds what they have today. Therefore, the major economic objective is to grow (and most assuredly maintain) the family fortune. This scenario is further complicated by the parameters some families put in place, such as:

- Equal shares to ALL family members
- Never touch the principle
- Transfer of wealth that incorporates lifestyle restrictions

When discussing this matter with family members, we find that it is useful to project out how long the family fortune as is will last if it did not increase or decrease due to investing. For the purposes of perspective, if you spent US $1,000 a day, it would take you about 2,740 years to spend US $1 billion. When we do financial projections with a family, we incorporate their current expenses as well as what they might do with the monies, which can include—as in one case—buying an island and building a castle on it. We also include some sort of increase in the number of inheritors.

This exercise is only intended to help family members think about the family fortune and if there is a need for it to grow. As noted, there are times there is enough money to last five generations. However, most of the time, we find that the successful family will need to continue to increase its wealth.

As part of this exercise, we calculate the return on investments needed to establish a family dynasty. In our experience, for most successful families to stay at an even plain may well require 10% to 25% annual compounding. This is a high benchmark for most of these families to maintain over the generations.

The Rationale for a Family Dynasty

If the family is seriously interested in establishing a family dynasty, you may very well be involved in helping think through what this means and help take steps to make it happen. If so, the perpetual question you need to ask for the establishment and continuity of a family dynasty is . . .

Why will the family members stay together?

There have to be strong reasons for the family members to be together generations from now. One way this is operationalized revolves around how the monies are managed. You can approach this matter by asking:

- What are the advantages of investing together?
- What are the disadvantages of investing together?
- Which way does the scale tip? Does it tip to the advantages side or to the disadvantages side?

Another important question the family has to answer is . . .

How should the family use its wealth?

Your aim is to help the family better define the purpose of the family fortune. There are no inherent right or wrong answers.

Instead, the goal is to find areas of consensus and ways to keep different family members constructively involved.

Along the same lines, the family needs to determine how it is going to empower future generations. For example, how will the family communicate its values and vision to heirs?

It is often a serious mistake to assume that family members will grow up and be able to take responsibility for the family fortune. It is much wiser to construct a clear path for heirs to become proficient and responsible. As an inner-circle single-family office senior executive, you will potentially be involved in preparing the heir to take ownership and control of the single-family office and ongoing family businesses.

Empowering Inheritors to Take Over

Inheritors must learn to take control of the processes that are core to sustaining and expanding their family dynasty. It is smart for the family to not completely rely on non-family members. While these various experts—when properly vetted—will do a top-notch job for the family, to them it is just their job.

Most of the time, the inheritors must learn to be stewards of their wealth and torchbearer of the family's values and beliefs. They need to learn to be responsible for themselves, their family, and their family legacy. This entails being involved in key decisions and learning to oversee the family's wealth and needs. In many families, being responsible also necessitates being able to build strong and optimal business relationships as well as skillfully leverage their own and the family's personal and business networks (see Appendix B).

Fostering capable: The requisite educational approach is geared intently around facilitating achievements. The focus of any viable educational program is to provide extraordinary and highly actionable curriculum that will enable family members to excel. It is this no-nonsense approach determined inheritors require and regularly demand.

The older generations and the inheritors are usually results-driven, and consequently, their education must also be results-proven. Time is a luxury few can afford. Education has to translate into accomplishments as fast as reasonably possible.

Theory, for instance, is nice and can certainly play a very important role in an inheritor's professional development. Theory can deliver insights and be effective in identifying opportunities and possibilities. But, for heirs looking to maintain and strengthen their family dynasties, theory alone is often limited and insufficient.

For theory to have maximum value in today's highly complicated and convoluted world, it must provide guidelines and backing for action. Thus, learning various theories without learning how to apply them is not as productive as possible. What these inheritors require is for theories to be tightly bound with competencies.

The following equation lays out the nature of the education dynamic inheritors require:

$$Applicable + Practical = Capable$$

Let us consider each of the components:

- **Applicable:** The educational content must be pertinent, relevant, and appropriate to the issues, resources, and situations the family members are facing or will face. Hence, there must be foundational material and more targeted content as part of a customizable curriculum such as issue-oriented material.

- **Practical:** The educational content must prepare the family members to efficaciously handle complex and conflict-ridden important matters as well as enable them to take on the mantle of stewardship. Furthermore, the educational content, where possible, should promote creativity and constructive cleverness. The world is dynamically changing, requiring that people quickly and meritoriously adapt.

- **Capable:** By adroitly ensuring the curriculum is *applicable* and *practical*, dedicated family members exit quite *capable*. They will have the knowledge and skills, the insights and proficiencies, to more efficaciously achieve high degrees of success. They will be able to make a significant positive difference in their families and in whatever endeavors they pursue. They will be able to further the family dynasty.

The future of a family dynasty rests on the shoulders of each successive generation. By ensuring inheritors are indeed capable, the family is doing the best it possibly can to perpetuate its legacy as well as a bright future for the current and future generations.

When You Are Family

Family members who are inner-circle single-family office senior executives tend to report that there is more pressure on them when the objective is to establish a family dynasty. Often, the family does not talk in these terms but will talk about their legacy and how future generations will benefit from what the family is doing today.

Realistically, few non-family senior executives will be that concerned with what circumstances will be like for your family a few generations out. Their self-interests almost always stop with their involvement with your single-family office. They are also less likely to know all the issues, concerns, and considerations your family is dealing with and how they impact future generations.

If a family dynasty is something your family thinks of as a possibility, then it is very likely that you will have to take responsibility for thinking strategically about what it is going to take to make it happen.

Conclusion

Across the world, a substantial number of families are aiming to create family dynasties. They are looking to perpetuate the values, beliefs, and wealth of the family for generations. High-performing single-family offices are powerful ways to help establish a family dynasty. They can play an important role in promoting family cohesiveness and in increasing the family wealth.

Most successful families find it necessary to grow the family wealth to create family dynasties. This is sometimes even the case when billion-dollar (US) fortunes are involved. It is all a function of the probable increase in the number of heirs and how the monies are currently being spent and invested.

In the end, however, for there to be a family dynasty, there have to be good reasons for the family to stay together. This situation is complicated with more family branches and more inheritors. At the same time, it is usually essential for heirs to be empowered. They need to learn to capably manage their legacy, including their family fortune.

For those families looking to establish family dynasties, your involvement as an inner-circle senior executive can be crucial. This is exponentially more the case when you are family.

Coda: The Future of the High-Performing Family Office

W E HAVE BEEN researching family offices, the wealthy, and professionals for decades. The following are some of the more pronounced trends we are seeing...

The wealthy are getting wealthier: While who is wealthy can vary—one person becoming a lot poorer while others becoming more affluent—overall, the wealthy are increasing in numbers and the amount of the world's wealth they control. Even during crises, the wealthy are expanding their lead from the rest of the population.

There are structural reasons for much of this disparity. Still, the gap between the *haves* and *have nots* is widening at a very fast clip. More telling is that the gap between the *haves* and *have yachts* is also precipitously widening.

The wealthy will continue to rely on the expertise of exceptional professionals: To navigate the tax code, to construct the optimal investment portfolios under varying circumstances, to insulate themselves from the likes of predators looking to weaponize the legal system, the wealthy have and will continue to turn to leading private wealth experts for solutions. The key is to be able to source and effectively work with talented, erudite, and skilled professionals.

There will be a proliferation of single-family and multi-family offices: The growth in private wealth coupled with a reliance on exceptional professionals will translate into more and more single-family offices. Very likely, at a faster rate, the number of multi-family offices will boom.

Families across the wealth spectrum are realizing that the family office promise—superior results—is hard to pass up. So, the very wealthy will usually choose a single-family office. For those less affluent, there are different versions of multi-family offices—and more on the way—that will fit their needs and wants cost-effectively.

High-performing family offices will become increasingly normative: Today, most single-family and multi-family offices are not high-performing (as we have defined the term). In a great many cases, for instance, the focus of the family office is on what they can do as opposed to addressing the self-interest of the families.

Successful families, for example, are becoming more and more aware of the possibilities, and when they are cognizant of their options, they insist their family offices are high-performing or they will take corrective actions. The same is likely to happen when it comes to less affluent individuals and families. People are disinclined to settle for less, especially when more is available.

High-performing family offices are totally dependent on inner-circle senior executives: You and your peers are the determining factor in whether a family office will be high-performing or not. Critically, your ability to understand the self-interests of family members, to marshal the requisite resources on their behalf, and to manage systematically differentiates high-performing family offices from those that fail to make the grade.

Your ability to fulfill the family office promise not only benefits the family but can majorly benefit you as well. Keeping your self-interests in mind, you will be able to better communicate the value you provide, which you can convert into greater personal wealth.

With considerable confidence in the likelihood of these trends, we readily recognize we are dealing with a rapidly moving target. Successful families and their supportive ecosystem are extremely adaptable. As the world of private wealth transforms, so will family offices.

APPENDICES

APPENDIX A

Researching Successful Families and Inner-Circle Single-Family Office Senior Executives

OUR RECOMMENDATIONS ON how to build a high-performing single-family office are derived from extensive experience educating, consulting, and coaching family members and senior executives. Supporting our work in the field is extensive empirical research.

We have employed two types of research methodologies to benchmark and determine the best practices of family offices. One approach is ethnography and the other approach is surveying.

Ethnography is used to better understand successful families. While it would be great to be able to survey family members, doing so is often not an option. On the other hand, surveying inner-circle senior executives in single-family offices is very doable. The survey research can sometimes, depending on the respondents and how the surveys are constructed, act as a proxy for surveying family members.

Let us take a closer look at each of the two research methodologies.

Two Research Methodologies

Social scientists rely on ethnographic research to learn about distinct and separate segments of societies in their natural environments. The social scientists will develop detailed case analyses that aim to explain the behaviors of a cohort as well as the results of those behaviors.

When it comes to successful families with single-family offices, the viable approaches are participant observation and interviews. Participant observation is when we have first-hand observations of the family engaging in various activities related to specific research questions. This does not happen very often.

Very, very few successful families are comfortable permitting strangers unfiltered access to their lives. This is all the more the case when those strangers are looking to evaluate them in some way and share their insights.

What proves much more effective are structured and unstructured interviews with family members. Even then there are lots of caveats, such as what is on and off the record. Still, as trust develops, family members tend to be willing to share more and share without censoring themselves.

While we have conducted ethnographic research with inner-circle single-family office executives, most of the insights we have derived from their cohort have been gathered by surveys. Unless they are family members, the senior executives are not comparably wealthy. As we discussed in Chapter 8, they are primarily talented and motivated professionals choosing to work in a single-family office. As such, they regularly respond to surveys. Respondents of surveys sent to single-family offices are business-to-business surveys.

Survey sampling: Constructing a sample is the most challenging and complicated part of researching single-family offices, as it is necessary to gain access to knowledgeable participants. All such research involves purposeful samples. Moreover, chain-referral sampling, as well as introductions from professionals they have engaged, is regularly a requisite when "studying up."

Another issue in surveying single-family office senior executives is the use of the information. Those responding are comfortable with aggregate results. Various forms of confidentiality agreements addressing the way the information they provided can be used are increasingly being required by the participants.

Using the Research

We did not cite research findings in this book, as our goal is to provide you with actionable guidelines and processes. Still, it is worthwhile to know the underlying basis for our recommendations as well as the limitations when researching these cohorts.

To be completely transparent, all empirical investigations in this arena are flawed. You therefore have to be careful when using the data to work with any particular single-family office. There is also the problem of extrapolating the research findings to the larger single-family office universe. The way the sample is constructed coupled with limited sample sizes can justifiably lead to questioning the accuracy of the findings.

It is therefore useful to look at ALL the research done in the field to get a better and more accurate understanding of successful families and single-family offices. Exhibit A summarizes the limitations of quantitative research with single-family offices.

EXHIBIT A: Complications in Researching Single-Family Offices

Issue	Limitation Example
Unknown size of universe	Impossible to obtain a random sample
Chain-referral sampling and introductions from professionals	Inherent bias due to referral sources
Surrogate respondents	Unable to discern the interpretive accuracy of the respondents' answers

It is critical to recognize that studying up is replete with a multitude of complications. All such research needs to be seen as adding to the discussion and not as definitive.

APPENDIX B

Personal Wealth Creation Coaching

T HE EVERYONE WINS Process is a cornerstone to the burgeoning field of personal wealth creation coaching. This form of coaching is in growing demand by the likes of successful families, and by fast-tracking entrepreneurs and talented professionals.

To create a sizable personal fortune or meaningfully grow an already substantial personal fortune, the ability to optimize or enhance business networks and business relationships is essential. The use of the Everyone Wins Process is therefore critical.

The Nature of Personal Wealth Creation Coaching

There is a growing number of coaches focusing on personal wealth creation. For the most part, these wealth creation authorities are focused on how you need to think (your mindset) and what you need to do (your skillset) in order to amass greater personal wealth. All personal wealth creation coaches share two important methodologies:

- **They all use some version of the Everyone Wins Process:** There is a common emphasis on strengthening business relationships and finding ways to work more productively with others, so everyone excels.

- **They all focus on providing guidance on how to grow and optimize professional and personal networks:** The ability to leverage and grow business networks is crucial to creating opportunities that translate into greater financial accomplishments.

While the two methodologies are appropriate in all situations, there are different applications. Specifically, there are three primary scenarios for personal wealth creation coaching (Exhibit B).

EXHIBIT B: Three Scenarios for Personal Wealth Creation Coaching

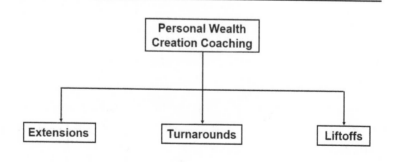

Extensions: This is where people are looking to become substantially wealthier. For example, a business owner worth US $500 million is seeking to become a billionaire. His personal wealth creation coaching was strongly predicated on leveraging his key business relationships and adroitly sharing his business acumen. His ability to help those in his business network by putting them in touch with other business owners and professionals was the basis of the extraordinary value he was able to deliver.

Turnarounds: Some people were once extremely wealthy but for various reasons lost a substantial portion of their fortunes. Now they want to regain their wealth. An example of this is a business owner who led a high-living celebrity lifestyle that both ate up his US $40 million net-worth and contributed to his sending his company into bankruptcy. While he antagonized some people as he flew too close to the sun, most of his business relationships were still quite solid. His coaching involved significantly strengthening and leveraging many of the business relationships he amassed over 25 years. By carefully choosing which relationships to enhance and which to optimize, he has been able to reestablish himself and now is fast-tracking the success of his new company.

Liftoffs: Some people have amassed some personal wealth and are striving for more, but they have, in one way or another, hit a ceiling and need some guidance. There is a highly successful business owner worth around US $25 million who wants to build a great fortune so he can underwrite research for a cure for pancreatic cancer (which caused the death of his son). His altruistic nature is working against him in dramatic ways. The focus of his personal wealth creation coaching is how to align his self-interests with those of the people he is dealing with and not "give away the store." This usually requires strategizing each important business negotiation using the Everyone Wins Process.

Criteria to Receive the Most Benefit from Personal Wealth Creation Coaching

Not everyone who desires greater affluence is a good candidate for personal wealth creation coaching. Simply put, the best candidates have certain qualities:

- A tremendous desire to excel and become much wealthier
- The mindset, talents, and skills that can be refined and refocused on what it is going to take to extend, fast-track, or rebuild a personal fortune
- The desire to approach business ethically, with the aim of helping all involved to achieve their self-interests
- A fairly extensive professional and/or personal network to enhance and monetize
- Financial or other resources (e.g., intellectual capital, existing businesses, etc.) that can be innovatively leveraged
- A willingness to listen and try

If you are seeking coaching to help you build your own personal fortune, some professionals can be helpful. However, you must be careful in selecting who to engage. Some personal wealth creation coaches are well-meaning but are just not up to the job. The right well-qualified personal wealth creation coach can prove very supportive and provide you with a tremendous education as well as a toolkit of processes and techniques that can prove invaluable in helping you create a considerable personal fortune.

CPSIA information can be obtained
at www.ICGtesting.com
Printed in the USA
BVHW091123100522
636626BV00001B/13

9 781662 907388